OVID'S AMORES

OVID'S AMORES

English Translation by
GUY LEE

with Latin Text

*

JOHN MURRAY

Printed in Great Britain for
John Murray, Albemarle Street, London
by William Clowes & Sons Ltd
London and Beccles

CASED EDITION: 7195 1796 6
PAPER EDITION: 7195 1805 9

CONTENTS

Book I   2–55

Book II   58–115

Book III   118–179

Notes   181

The Poet   195

The Translation   199

Acknowledgements   202

Wood engraving of myrtle by Reynolds Stone

EPIGRAMMA IPSIVS

Qui modo Nasonis fueramus quinque libelli
   tres sumus: hoc illi praetulit auctor opus.
ut iam nulla tibi nos sit legisse voluptas
   at levior demptis poena duobus erit

AUTHOR'S NOTE

Once five, now three slim volumes
we are Naso's preference.
Even if we give no pleasure
the pain will be two books less.

BOOK I

i

Arma gravi numero violentaque bella parabam
    edere, materia conveniente modis.

par erat inferior versus: risisse Cupido
    dicitur atque unum surripuisse pedem.

'quis tibi, saeve puer, dedit hoc in carmina iuris?
    Pieridum vates, non tua, turba sumus.

quid si praeripiat flavae Venus arma Minervae,
    ventilet accensas flava Minerva faces?

quis probet in silvis Cererem regnare iugosis,
    lege pharetratae virginis arva coli?

crinibus insignem quis acuta cuspide Phoebum
    instruat, Aoniam Marte movente lyram?

sunt tibi magna, puer, nimiumque potentia regna.
    cur opus adfectas, ambitiose, novum?

an quod ubique tuum est? tua sunt Heliconia tempe?
    vix etiam Phoebo iam lyra tuta sua est?

cum bene surrexit versu nova pagina primo,
    attenuat nervos proximus ille meos.

nec mihi materia est numeris levioribus apta—
    aut puer aut longas compta puella comas.'

questus eram, pharetra cum protinus ille soluta
    legit in exitium spicula facta meum

lunavitque genu sinuosum fortiter arcum
    'quod'que 'canas, vates, accipe' dixit 'opus.'

me miserum, certas habuit puer ille sagittas.
    uror et in vacuo pectore regnat Amor.

sex mihi surgat opus numeris, in quinque residat.
    ferrea cum vestris bella valete modis.

i

My epic was under construction—wars and armed violence
in the grand manner, with metre matching theme.
I had written the second hexameter when Cupid grinned
and calmly removed one of its feet.

'You young savage' I protested 'poetry's none of your business.
We poets are committed to the Muses.

Imagine Venus grabbing Minerva's armour
and Minerva brandishing love's torch!

Imagine Ceres queen of the mountain forests
and Diana the huntress running a farm!

Or longhaired Phoebus doing pike drill
and Mars strumming the seven-stringed lyre!

You've a large empire, my boy—too much power already.
Why so eager for extra work?

Or is the whole world yours—the glens of Helicon included?
Can't Phoebus call his lyre his own these days?

Page one line one of my epic rises to noble heights
but line two lowers the tone

and I haven't the right subject for light verse—
a pretty boy or a girl with swept-up hair.'

In reply the god undid his quiver and pulled out
an arrow with my name on it.

'Poet' he said, flexing the bow against his knee,
'I'll give you something to sing about—take that!'

Alas his arrows never miss. My blood's on fire.
Love has moved in as master of my heart.

I choose the couplet—rising six feet, falling five.
Farewell, hexameters and iron wars.

cingere litorea flaventia tempora myrto,
    Musa per undenos emodulanda pedes.

ii

Esse quid hoc dicam, quod tam mihi dura videntur
    strata neque in lecto pallia nostra sedent,

et vacuus somno noctem, quam longa, peregi
    lassaque versati corporis ossa dolent?

nam puto sentirem si quo temptarer amore—
    an subit et tecta callidus arte nocet?

sic erit. haeserunt tenues in corde sagittae
    et possessa ferus pectora versat Amor.

cedimus? an subitum luctando accendimus ignem?
    cedamus. leve fit quod bene fertur onus.

vidi ego iactatas mota face crescere flammas
    et vidi nullo concutiente mori.

verbera plura ferunt quam quos iuvat usus aratri,
    detractant prensi dum iuga prima boves.

asper equus duris contunditur ora lupatis;
    frena minus sentit quisquis ad arma facit.

acrius invitos multoque ferocius urget
    quam qui servitium ferre fatentur Amor.

en ego confiteor—tua sum nova praeda, Cupido.
    porrigimus victas ad tua iura manus.

nil opus est bello; veniam pacemque rogamus,
    nec tibi laus armis victus inermis ero.

necte comam myrto. maternas iunge columbas.
    qui deceat currum vitricus ipse dabit,

inque dato curru, populo clamante Triumphum,
    stabis et adiunctas arte movebis aves.

AMORES I i 29–ii 26

Garland your golden hair with myrtle from the seaside,
hendecametric Muse, my Elegia.

ii

What's wrong with me I wonder? This mattress feels so hard.
The blankets won't stay on the bed.

I haven't slept a wink—tossing and turning
all night long. And now I'm aching all over.

Can it be love? Surely I'd know if it were?
Or does love work under cover and strike unobserved?

Yes, those phantom arrows must have pierced my heart
and relentless Cupid is torturing me.

Shall I give in? Or fan the flame by fighting it?
Better give in. Balance makes a burden light.

Shake a torch and it flares up—
leave it alone and it dies.

A bullock restive under the yoke
gets beaten more than his patient partner.

Spirited horses bruise their mouths on the bit;
the docile seldom feel it.

The god of love hits rebels far harder
than his submissive slaves.

Then I submit, Cupid. I'm your latest victim
standing here with my hands up.

The war's over. I'm suing for peace and pardon.
There's no glory in shooting an unarmed man.

Bind your hair with myrtle. Harness your mother's doves.
Vulcan will fit you out with a chariot.

Mount it and steer your doves through the crowd
as they hail you victor.

5

ducentur capti iuvenes captaeque puellae;
    haec tibi magnificus pompa triumphus erit.

ipse ego, praeda recens, factum modo vulnus habebo
    et nova captiva vincula mente feram.

Mens Bona ducetur manibus post terga retortis
    et Pudor et castris quidquid Amoris obest.

omnia te metuent. ad te sua bracchia tendens
    volgus *Io* magna voce *Triumphe* canet.

Blanditiae comites tibi erunt Errorque Furorque,
    adsidue partes turba secuta tuas.

his tu militibus superas hominesque deosque;
    haec tibi si demas commoda, nudus eris.

laeta triumphanti de summo mater Olympo
    plaudet et adpositas sparget in ora rosas.

tu pinnas gemma, gemma variante capillos,
    ibis in auratis aureus ipse rotis.

tunc quoque non paucos, si te bene novimus, ures;
    tunc quoque praeteriens vulnera multa dabis.

non possunt, licet ipse velis, cessare sagittae.
    fervida vicino flamma vapore nocet.

talis erat domita Bacchus Gangetide terra;
    tu gravis alitibus, tigribus ille fuit.

ergo cum possim sacri pars esse triumphi,
    parce tuas in me perdere victor opes.

aspice cognati felicia Caesaris arma:
    qua vicit victos protegit ille manu.

You too can celebrate a glorious Triumph
with young men and girls as your prisoners of war

and I'll be among them wearing my new chains
nursing this open wound—your abject slave.

Conscience and Common Sense and all Love's enemies
will be dragged along with hands tied behind their backs.

You'll strike fear into all hearts.
The crowd will worship you, chanting *Io Triumphe*.

Your loyal irregulars Flattery Passion and Illusion
will act as bodyguard,

the forces that bring you victory over gods and men,
providing cover for your nakedness.

Your laughing mother will watch the Triumph from Olympus
and clap her hands and shower you with roses

as you ride along, jewels flashing from wings and hair,
a golden boy in a golden chariot,

raising many a fire if I know you,
wounding many a heart as you pass by,

your arrows willy-nilly never resting,
the flame of your torch scorching at close range,

a god mighty as Bacchus along the Ganges,
your doves terrible as tigers.

Then spare me for your Triumph.
Don't waste your strength on me

but imitate your conquering cousin Augustus—
he turns his conquests into protectorates.

iii

Iusta precor. quae me nuper praedata puella est
  aut amet aut faciat cur ego semper amem.
a nimium volui. tantum patiatur amari—
  audierit nostras tot Cytherea preces.
accipe per longos tibi qui deserviat annos,
  accipe qui pura norit amare fide.
si me non veterum commendant magna parentum
  nomina, si nostri sanguinis auctor eques,
nec meus innumeris renovatur campus aratris,
  temperat et sumptus parcus uterque parens,
at Phoebus comitesque novem vitisque repertor
  hac faciunt, et me qui tibi donat Amor,
et nulli cessura fides, sine crimine mores,
  nudaque simplicitas purpureusque pudor.
non mihi mille placent, non sum desultor amoris.
  tu mihi, siqua fides, cura perennis eris.
tecum quos dederint annos mihi fila Sororum
  vivere contingat, teque dolente mori.
te mihi materiem felicem in carmina praebe—
  provenient causa carmina digna sua.
carmine nomen habent exterrita cornibus Io
  et quam fluminea lusit adulter ave
quaeque super pontum simulato vecta iuvenco
  virginea tenuit cornua vara manu.
nos quoque per totum pariter cantabimur orbem
  iunctaque semper erunt nomina nostra tuis.

iii

Thief of my heart, it's only fair
you should give me yours or cherish mine for ever.

No, I'm asking too much—simply let me love you
and Venus will have answered all my prayers.

I'll be your slave for life,
your ever faithful lover.

I can't claim noble ancestry,
my father's a mere knight,

my acres are hardly broad,
my allowance barely enough.

But Phoebus and the Nine are with me,
the wine-god and the god of love,

fidelity, integrity,
sincerity, sensitivity.

I'm no philanderer leaping from bed to bed.
I promise to be yours for ever.

O for the luck to live with you while life's thread lasts
and to die while you weep beside me!

You shall be theme and inspiration,
my verse the mirror of your merit.

Io the timid heifer,
Leda who loved a swan,

Europa at sea, holding tight to a bull's horns—
these owe fame to verse.

Verse can make *us* world-famous too,
linking our names—together always.

iv

Vir tuus est epulas nobis aditurus easdem?
    ultima cena tuo sit precor illa viro.

ergo ego dilectam tantum conviva puellam
    aspiciam? tangi quem iuvet alter erit?

alteriusque sinus apte subiecta fovebis?
    iniciet collo, cum volet, ille manum?

desine mirari posito quod candida vino
    Atracis ambiguos traxit in arma viros.

nec mihi silva domus nec equo mea membra cohaerent:
    vix a te videor posse tenere manus.

quae tibi sint facienda tamen cognosce, nec Euris
    da mea nec tepidis verba ferenda Notis.

ante veni quam vir—nec quid, si veneris ante,
    possit agi video, sed tamen ante veni.

cum premet ille torum, vultu comes ipsa modesto
    ibis ut accumbas, clam mihi tange pedem.

me specta nutusque meos vultumque loquacem.
    excipe furtivas et refer ipsa notas.

verba superciliis sine voce loquentia dicam,
    verba leges digitis, verba notata mero.

cum tibi succurret veneris lascivia nostrae,
    purpureas tenero pollice tange genas.

si quid erit de me tacita quod mente queraris,
    pendeat extrema mollis ab aure manus.

cum tibi quae faciam, mea lux, dicamve placebunt,
    versetur digitis anulus usque tuis.

tange manu mensam tangunt quo more precantes,
    optabis merito cum mala multa viro.

iv

Your husband? Going to the same dinner as us?
I hope it chokes him.

So I'm only to gaze at you, darling? Play gooseberry
while another man enjoys your touch?

You'll lie there snuggling up to him? He'll put his arm
round your neck whenever he wants?

No wonder Centaurs fought over Hippodamia
when the wedding wine began to flow.

I don't live in the forest nor am I part horse
but I find it hard to keep my hands off you.

However here's my plan. Listen carefully.
Don't throw my words of wisdom to the winds.

Arrive before him—not that I see what good
arriving first will do but arrive first all the same.

When he takes his place on the couch and you go to join him
looking angelic, secretly touch my foot.

Watch me for nods and looks that talk
and unobserved return my signals

in the language of eyebrows and fingers
with annotations in wine.

Whenever you think of our love-making
stroke that rosy cheek with your thumb.

If you're cross with me, darling,
press the lobe of your ear

but turn your ring round if you're pleased
with anything I say or do.

When you feel like cursing your fool of a husband
touch the table as if you were praying.

quod tibi miscuerit—sapias—bibat ipse iubeto;
   tu puerum leviter posce quod ipsa voles.

quae tu reddideris ego primus pocula sumam
   et qua tu biberis hac ego parte bibam.

si tibi forte dabit quod praegustaverit ipse,
   reice libatos illius ore cibos.

nec premat impositis sinito tua colla lacertis,
   mite nec in rigido pectore pone caput,

nec sinus admittat digitos habilesve papillae;
   oscula praecipue nulla dedisse velis.

oscula si dederis, fiam manifestus amator
   et dicam 'mea sunt' iniciamque manum.

haec tamen aspiciam, sed quae bene pallia celant,
   illa mihi caeci causa timoris erunt.

nec femori committe femur, nec crure cohaere,
   nec tenerum duro cum pede iunge pedem.

multa miser timeo quia feci multa proterve,
   exemplique metu torqueor ipse mei.

saepe mihi dominaeque meae properata voluptas
   veste sub iniecta dulce peregit opus.

hoc tu non facies—sed ne fecisse puteris
   conscia de tergo pallia deme tuo.

vir bibat usque roga (precibus tamen oscula desint)
   dumque bibit, furtim, si potes, adde merum.

si bene compositus somno vinoque iacebit,
   consilium nobis resque locusque dabunt.

cum surges abitura domum, surgemus et omnes,
   in medium turbae fac memor agmen eas.

agmine me invenies aut invenieris in illo;
   quidquid ibi poteris tangere tange mei.

me miserum, monui paucas quod prosit in horas.
   separor a domina nocte iubente mea.

AMORES I iv 29–60

If he mixes you a drink, beware—tell him to drink it himself,
then quietly ask the waiter for what you want.

I'll intercept the glass as you hand it back
and drink from the side you drank from.

Refuse all food he has tasted first—
it has touched his lips.

Don't lean your gentle head against his shoulder
and don't let him embrace you

or slide a hand inside your dress
or touch your breasts. Above all don't kiss him.

If you do I'll cause a public scandal,
grab you and claim possession.

I'm bound to see all this. It's what I shan't see
that worries me—the goings on under your cloak.

Don't press your thigh or your leg against his
or touch his coarse feet with your toes.

I know all the tricks. That's why I'm worried.
I hate to think of him doing what I've done.

We've often made love under your cloak, sweetheart,
in a glorious race against time.

You won't do that, I know. Still,
to avoid all doubt don't wear one.

Encourage him to drink but mind—no kisses.
Keep filling his glass when he's not looking.

If the wine's too much for him and he drops off
we can take our cue from what's going on around us.

When you get up to leave and we all follow
move to the middle of the crowd.

You'll find me there—or I'll find you
so touch me anywhere you can.

But what's the good? I'm only temporizing.
Tonight decrees our separation.

13

nocte vir includet. lacrimis ego maestus obortis,
    qua licet, ad saevas prosequar usque fores.

oscula iam sumet, iam non tantum oscula sumet—
    quod mihi das furtim iure coacta dabis.

verum invita dato—potes hoc—similisque coactae.
    blanditiae taceant sitque maligna Venus.

si mea vota valent, illum quoque ne iuvet opto.
    si minus, at certe te iuvet inde nihil.

sed quaecumque tamen noctem fortuna sequetur,
    cras mihi constanti voce dedisse nega.

V

Aestus erat, mediamque dies exegerat horam.
    adposui medio membra levanda toro.

pars adaperta fuit, pars altera clausa fenestrae,
    quale fere silvae lumen habere solent,

qualia sublucent fugiente crepuscula Phoebo
    aut ubi nox abiit nec tamen orta dies.

illa verecundis lux est praebenda puellis,
    qua timidus latebras speret habere pudor.

ecce, Corinna venit, tunica velata recincta,
    candida dividua colla tegente coma,

qualiter in thalamos formosa Sameramis isse
    dicitur et multis Lais amata viris.

deripui tunicam—nec multum rara nocebat,
    pugnabat tunica sed tamen illa tegi.

quae cum ita pugnaret tamquam quae vincere nollet,
    victa est non aegre proditione sua.

ut stetit ante oculos posito velamine nostros,
    in toto nusquam corpore menda fuit.

Tonight he'll lock you in and leave me
desolated at your door.

Then he'll kiss you, then go further,
forcing his right to our secret joy.

But you *can* show him you're acting under duress.
Be mean with your love—give grudgingly—in silence.

He won't enjoy it if my prayers are answered.
And if they're not, at least assure me you won't.

But whatever happens tonight tell me tomorrow
you didn't sleep with him—and stick to that story.

V

Siesta time in sultry summer.
I lay relaxed on the divan.

One shutter closed, the other ajar,
made sylvan semi-darkness,

a glimmering dusk, as after sunset,
or between night's end and day's beginning—

the half light shy girls need
to hide their hesitation.

At last—Corinna. On the loose in a short dress,
long hair parted and tumbling past the pale neck—

lovely as Lais of the many lovers,
Queen Semiramis gliding in.

I grabbed the dress; it didn't hide much,
but she fought to keep it,

only half-heartedly though.
Victory was easy, a self-betrayal.

There she stood, faultless beauty
in front of me, naked.

quos umeros, quales vidi tetigique lacertos!
　　forma papillarum quam fuit apta premi!
quam castigato planus sub pectore venter!
　　quantum et quale latus! quam iuvenale femur!
singula quid referam? nil non laudabile vidi,
　　et nudam pressi corpus ad usque meum.
cetera quis nescit? lassi requievimus ambo.
　　proveniant medii sic mihi saepe dies.

vi

Ianitor—indignum!—dura religate catena,
　　difficilem moto cardine pande forem.
quod precor exiguum est. aditu fac ianua parvo
　　obliquum capiat semiadaperta latus.
longus amor tales corpus tenuavit in usus
　　aptaque subducto corpore membra dedit.
ille per excubias custodum leniter ire
　　monstrat, inoffensos derigit ille pedes.
at quondam noctem simulacraque vana timebam.
　　mirabar tenebris quisquis iturus erat.
risit ut audirem tenera cum matre Cupido
　　et leviter 'fies tu quoque fortis' ait,
nec mora, venit amor. non umbras nocte volantis,
　　non timeo strictas in mea fata manus.
te nimium lentum timeo. tibi blandior uni.
　　tu me quo possis perdere fulmen habes.
aspice—uti videas immitia claustra relaxa—
　　uda sit ut lacrimis ianua facta meis.
certe ego, cum posita stares ad verbera veste,
　　ad dominam pro te verba tremente tuli.

Shoulders and arms challenging eyes and fingers.
Nipples firmly demanding attention.

Breasts in high relief above the smooth belly.
Long and slender waist. Thighs of a girl.

Why list perfection?
I hugged her tight.

The rest can be imagined—we fell asleep.
Such afternoons are rare.

vi

Porter!—poor wretch, chained like a dog—
please open up.

I don't ask much—a mere crack
so there's room to squeeze through sideways.

Love has made me slim enough,
halved my weight and alerted my limbs.

He can teach you to slip past sentries—
never lets you put a foot wrong.

I used to be scared of the dark—
admired people who went out at night.

But Cupid and his mother, laughing in my ear,
whispered 'You too can be brave'

and brought me love. I'm not afraid of ghosts now
or hands raised to strike me down.

It's only you I'm frightened of. You're so slow.
It's only you who make me crawl. Your bolt can destroy me.

Just look at this door. Unbar it so you can see.
It's all wet with my tears.

That day you were stripped for a whipping—remember?—
I got your mistress to let you off.

ergo quae valuit pro te quoque gratia quondam—
  heu facinus!—pro me nunc valet illa parum?

redde vicem meritis. grato licet esse quod optas.
  tempora noctis eunt. excute poste seram.

excute, sic umquam longa relevere catena
  nec tibi perpetuo serva bibatur aqua.

ferreus orantem nequiquam, ianitor, audis;
  roboribus duris ianua fulta riget.

urbibus obsessis clausae munimina portae
  prosunt: in media pace quid arma times?

quid facies hosti, qui sic excludis amantem?
  tempora noctis eunt. excute poste seram.

non ego militibus venio comitatus et armis.
  solus eram si non saevus adesset Amor.

hunc ego, si cupiam, nusquam dimittere possum;
  ante vel a membris dividar ipse meis.

ergo Amor et modicum circa mea tempora vinum
  mecum est et madidis lapsa corona comis.

arma quis haec timeat? quis non eat obvius illis?
  tempora noctis eunt. excute poste seram.

lentus es? an somnus—qui te male perdat!—amantis
  verba dat in ventos aure repulsa tua?

at memini primo, cum te celare volebam,
  pervigil in mediae sidera noctis eras.

forsitan et tecum tua nunc requiescit amica.
  heu melior quanto sors tua sorte mea!

dummodo sic, in me durae transite catenae.
  tempora noctis eunt. excute poste seram.

fallimur an verso sonuerunt cardine postes,
  raucaque concussae signa dedere fores?

fallimur. impulsa est animoso ianua vento.
  ei mihi quam longe spem tulit aura meam!

I helped you then and now you won't help me.
Do you call that fair?

One good turn deserves another. Now's your chance to thank me.
The night is slipping by. Unbar the door.

And soon you'll be rid of your long chain,
drinking the wine of freedom at last . . .

Porter, you're hard. You can hear me pleading
but this heavy door hasn't moved an inch.

Beleaguered cities bar their gates.
But why be afraid of weapons in peacetime?

Lock out lovers and what have you left for enemies?
The night is slipping by. Unbar the door.

I'm not here with an armed guard—
I'd be alone if cruel Love weren't with me.

I could never dismiss *him*—
I'd have to be dismembered first.

So there's me, and Love, and a little wine (gone to my head),
and a garland askew on my damp hair.

Who's afraid of an outfit like that? Who wouldn't welcome it?
The night is slipping by. Unbar the door.

Perhaps you're asleep, damn you,
and my words aren't sinking in.

But you stayed awake till starry midnight
in the old days when I tried to slip out.

Or have you a girl-friend in your cell?
If so you're better off than me.

To be with mine I'd gladly wear your chain.
The night is slipping by. Unbar the door.

Listen! Did those hinges creak?
Was that something hitting the door? . . .

Only a gust of wind against it
blowing my poor hopes out of reach.

19

si satis es raptae, Borea, memor Orithyiae,
    huc ades et surdas flamine tunde foris.

urbe silent tota vitreoque madentia rore
    tempora noctis eunt. excute poste seram.

aut ego iam ferroque ignique paratior ipse
    quem face sustineo tecta superba petam.

nox et Amor vinumque nihil moderabile suadent.
    illa pudore vacat, Liber Amorque metu.

omnia consumpsi, nec te precibusque minisque
    movimus, o foribus durior ipse tuis!

non te formosae decuit servare puellae
    limina. sollicito carcere dignus eras.

iamque pruinosos molitur Lucifer axes,
    inque suum miseros excitat ales opus.

at tu, non laetis detracta corona capillis,
    dura super tota limina nocte iace.

tu dominae, cum te proiectam mane videbit,
    temporis absumpti tam male testis eris.

qualiscumque vale sentique abeuntis honorem,
    lente nec admisso turpis amante—vale.

vos quoque, crudeles rigido cum limine postes
    duraque conservae ligna, valete, fores.

vii

Adde manus in vincla meas—meruere catenas—
    dum furor omnis abit, si quis amicus ades.

nam furor in dominam temeraria bracchia movit.
    flet mea vesana laesa puella manu.

tunc ego vel caros potui violare parentes
    saeva vel in sanctos verbera ferre deos.

Ah Boreas, if you still remember the bride you ravished
blow this way and bang on these deaf panels . . .

Silence in Rome, and bright dew falling,
and *night slipping by. Unbar the door.*

Or I'll use my torch's fire and steel
to teach this lordly house a lesson.

Night and wine and love can't abide half measures.
Love and wine are fearless. Night has no shame . . .

I've tried everything. Threats and entreaties are useless.
This oak has a softer heart than yours.

Guarding the door of a pretty girl?
You ought to be a prison warder.

And now the morning star looms in a frosty sky.
Cocks are crowing to wake the world's workers.

I'm out of luck. I'll pull this garland off my head
and throw it down on the doorstep.

My love will see it lying there
in token of a wasted night.

Meanwhile, you oafish locker-out of lovers,
I do you the honour of saying goodbye.

You too, stone steps, deaf posts, and wooden door,
goodbye—and thanks for your servility.

vii

Tie up my hands, any friend of mine here,
tie them up till I'm sane again—they deserve it.

In a fit of madness I hit my love,
hurt her and made her cry.

In that state I could have hit my own mother
or taken a whip to the holy gods.

quid? non et clipei dominus septemplicis Aiax
    stravit deprensos lata per arva greges?
et vindex in matre, patris malus ultor, Orestes
    ausus in arcanas poscere tela deas?
ergo ego digestos potui laniare capillos?
    nec dominam motae dedecuere comae.
sic formosa fuit. talem Schoeneida dicam
    Maenalias arcu sollicitasse feras.
talis periuri promissaque velaque Thesei
    flevit praecipites Cressa tulisse Notos.
sic nisi vittatis quod erat Cassandra capillis
    procubuit templo, casta Minerva, tuo.
quis mihi non 'demens', quis non mihi 'barbare' dixit?
    ipsa nihil. pavido est lingua retenta metu.
sed taciti fecere tamen convicia vultus.
    egit me lacrimis ore silente reum.
ante meos umeris vellem cecidisse lacertos;
    utiliter potui parte carere mei.
in mea vesanas habui dispendia vires,
    et valui poenam fortis in ipse meam.
quid mihi vobiscum, caedis scelerumque ministrae?
    debita sacrilegae vincla subite manus.
an si pulsassem minimum de plebe Quiritem,
    plecterer, in dominam ius mihi maius erit?
pessima Tydides scelerum monimenta reliquit:
    ille deam primus perculit—alter ego.
at minus ille nocens. mihi quam profitebar amare
    laesa est; Tydides saevus in hoste fuit.
i nunc, magnificos victor molire triumphos,
    cinge comam lauro votaque redde Iovi,
quaeque tuos currus comitantum turba sequetur
    clamet 'io, forti victa puella viro est!'

I was mad as Homeric Ajax
when he massacred the flocks,

mad as Orestes the matricide
when he threatened to fight the Furies.

How could I do it? How could I ravel that perfect hair?
Yet ravelled hair became her—

she still looked lovely, like Atalanta
shooting beasts in Arcadia,

or Ariadne in tears while the south wind
blew Theseus and his promises away,

or Cassandra kneeling at Athena's altar,
except that *she* was wearing a headband.

'Crazy brute!' I can hear you saying
but she said nothing—she was too afraid.

Her eyes were my accusation though
and I read my sentence in her tears.

I'd sooner my arms had dropped from their sockets—
I'd have done better without them.

Victim of my own violence
I used a madman's strength to punish myself.

These hands are instruments of crime and bloodshed—
guilty of sacrilege. Chain them up.

If I struck the humblest citizen I'd pay for it:
have I any more right to strike my mistress?

Diomede set an evil precedent:
he was the first man to wound a goddess—and I'm the second.

But he had more excuse. He was fighting an enemy.
I hurt the girl I professed to love.

Come on, conquering hero, get ready for your Triumph.
Wear your laurels and give God the glory.

There'll be a fine procession all shouting
'Hurrah for the hero who beat his girl!'

ante eat effuso tristis captiva capillo,
  si sinerent laesae, candida tota, genae.

aptius impressis fuerat livere labellis
  et collum blandi dentis habere notam.

denique si tumidi ritu torrentis agebar
  caecaque me praedam fecerat ira suam,

nonne satis fuerat timidae inclamasse puellae
  nec nimium rigidas intonuisse minas?

aut tunicam a summa diducere turpiter ora
  ad mediam?—mediae zona tulisset opem.

at nunc sustinui raptis a fronte capillis
  ferreus ingenuas ungue notare genas.

astitit illa amens, albo et sine sanguine vultu,
  caeduntur Pariis qualia saxa iugis.

exanimes artus et membra trementia vidi
  ut cum populeas ventilat aura comas,

aut leni Zephyro gracilis vibratur harundo,
  summave cum tepido stringitur unda Noto.

suspensaeque diu, lacrimae fluxere per ora
  qualiter abiecta de nive manat aqua.

tunc ego me primum coepi sentire nocentem.
  sanguis erat lacrimae quas dabat illa meus.

ter tamen ante pedes volui procumbere supplex;
  ter formidatas reppulit illa manus.

at tu ne dubita—minuet vindicta dolorem—
  protinus in vultus unguibus ire meos.

nec nostris oculis nec nostris parce capillis—
  quamlibet infirmas adiuvat ira manus.

neve mei sceleris tam tristia signa supersint,
  pone recompositas in statione comas.

She'll walk in front, a poor prisoner, with ravelled hair,
pale as a ghost, except for the bruises on her cheeks.

I'd rather her neck were marked
black and blue with love-bites.

If I had to give way to a flood of rage,
to blind fury,

couldn't I merely have shouted and stormed
to frighten her—not too much?

Or ripped her dress down to the waist
where the belt would have saved it?

But no. I behaved like a brute,
grabbing her hair, scratching her cheeks.

She stood there dazed. Her face
went white as Parian marble.

Her body froze, but I could see her trembling
like aspen leaves in a breath of air

or slender reeds when the breeze blows softly
or water ruffled by a summer wind.

Her tears welled up, hung there, and at last brimmed over
like snow melting.

It was then I knew what I had done—
those tears were my life-blood.

Three times I tried to clasp her feet and beg forgiveness,
three times she pushed my hands away—terrified.

Don't wait, my dear. Revenge is sweet.
Dig your nails in my face—now.

Show my hair and my eyes no mercy.
Anger will give you strength.

Or at least remove the grim evidence of my crime
and discipline that wild hair again.

viii

Est quaedam—quicumque volet cognoscere lenam
  audiat—est quaedam nomine Dipsas anus.

ex re nomen habet. nigri non illa parentem
  Memnonis in roseis sobria vidit equis.

illa magas artes Aeaeaque carmina novit
  inque caput liquidas arte recurvat aquas.

scit bene quid gramen, quid torto concita rhombo
  licia, quid valeat virus amantis equae.

cum voluit, toto glomerantur nubila caelo;
  cum voluit, puro fulget in orbe dies.

sanguine, si qua fides, stillantia sidera vidi;
  purpureus Lunae sanguine vultus erat.

hanc ego nocturnas versam volitare per umbras
  suspicor et pluma corpus anile tegi—

suspicor et fama est. oculis quoque pupula duplex
  fulminat et gemino lumen ab orbe venit.

evocat antiquis proavos atavosque sepulcris
  et solidam longo carmine findit humum.

haec sibi proposuit thalamos temerare pudicos;
  nec tamen eloquio lingua nocente caret.

fors me sermoni testem dedit. illa monebat
  talia (me duplices occuluere fores):

'scis here te, mea lux, iuveni placuisse beato?
  haesit et in vultu constitit usque tuo.

et cur non placeas? nulli tua forma secunda est.
  me miseram, dignus corpore cultus abest.

tam felix esses quam formosissima vellem.
  non ego te facta divite pauper ero.

viii

There's someone I know—if you want to meet a Madam read on—
there's an old bitch I know called Dipsas.

What better name for her? Rosy Dawn
has never seen her sober.

She's the local witch—
can reverse the flow of water,

whirl the magic wheel, cull herbs,
brew aphrodisiacs,

guarantee the weather,
cloud or sunshine,

blood red stars (believe it or not)
or a bloody moon—I've seen both.

She's a night-bird—probably flits about
in owlish feathers.

That's what people say. And her eyes
are twin-pupilled, glinting double.

She's necromantic too
and chants earth-splitting spells.

Well, this creature tried to corrupt my innocent girl
and she's very persuasive—poisonously so.

The door was open. I happened to overhear
the following lecture:

'You know, my dear, you made quite a hit yesterday
with that rich young man. He couldn't take his eyes off you.

And no wonder. You're beautiful—no one more so.
It's such a pity you don't make the most of yourself.

I want that lovely face to be your fortune—
I know you'd never let old Dipsas starve.

stella tibi oppositi nocuit contraria Martis.
    Mars abiit; signo nunc Venus apta suo.

prosit ut adveniens en aspice! dives amator
    te cupiit. curae quid tibi desit habet.

est etiam facies qua se tibi conparet illi.
    si te non emptam vellet, emendus erat.

erubuit! decet alba quidem pudor ora. sed iste
    si simules prodest; verus obesse solet.

cum bene deiectis gremium spectabis ocellis,
    quantum quisque ferat respiciendus erit.

forsitan immundae Tatio regnante Sabinae
    noluerint habiles pluribus esse viris.

nunc Mars externis animos exercet in armis,
    at Venus Aeneae regnat in urbe sui.

ludunt formosae. casta est quam nemo rogavit,
    aut si rusticitas non vetat, ipsa rogat.

has quoque quae frontis rugas in vertice portant
    excute: de rugis crimina multa cadent.

Penelope iuvenum vires temptabat in arcu;
    qui latus argueret corneus arcus erat.

labitur occulte fallitque volatilis aetas,
    et celer admissis labitur annus equis.

aera nitent usu, vestis bona quaerit haberi,
    canescunt turpi tecta relicta situ.

forma, nisi admittas, nullo exercente senescit.
    nec satis effectus unus et alter habent.

certior e multis nec tam invidiosa rapina est;
    plena venit canis de grege praeda lupis.

ecce, quid iste tuus praeter nova carmina vates
    donat? amatoris milia multa leges.

ipse deus vatum palla spectabilis aurea
    tractat inauratae consona fila lyrae.

With Mars in opposition the luck was against you
but Venus in Libra has turned the golden scale

and look how your luck has changed! Here's a rich lover
pining to satisfy your every need!

He's handsome too—almost as pretty as you are.
If he weren't so keen to buy *you* we'd have to buy *him*.

She's blushing!—Yes, modesty suits a pale skin
but it's better put on—the real thing can be a nuisance.

You must look demurely down at your lap and ration your glances
to suit the value of each lover's gift.

I know those Sabine frumps refused to be obliging
but that was in King Tatius' bad old days.

Today Mars is kept so busy fighting abroad
that Venus has things all her own way in Rome.

Pretty girls play. Chaste means never asked.
If you're really smart you do your own asking.

Those girls that hold up their hands in horror—
look at them closer—they're praying for a lover.

Even Penelope sized up her suitors—
got them to draw that bow of horn.

Time slips past. We don't notice it passing
but the years slip by at a gallop.

It's use that makes bronze shine. Pretty dresses need wearing.
Neglected property falls to rack and ruin.

Your beauty needs exercise. It will soon fade
if you don't take lovers—and one or two aren't enough.

Best have a crowd to fleece, like the grey wolf.
It's a surer way and much less obvious.

Now take the poet of yours—he sends you his collections
but you'd collect far more from a proper lover.

Poets ought to be rich. Apollo their patron god
wears cloth of gold and twangs a golden lyre.

29

qui dabit, ille tibi magno sit maior Homero.
  crede mihi, res est ingeniosa dare.
nec tu si quis erit capitis mercede redemptus
  despice. gypsati crimen inane pedis.
nec te decipiant veteres circum atria cerae.
  tolle tuos tecum, pauper amator, avos.
qui quia pulcher erit poscet sine munere noctem,
  quod det amatorem flagitet ante suum.
parcius exigito pretium dum retia tendis,
  ne fugiant. captos legibus ure tuis.
nec nocuit simulatus amor. sine credat amari
  et cave ne gratis hic tibi constet amor.
saepe nega noctes. capitis modo finge dolorem,
  et modo quae causas praebeat Isis erit.
mox recipe, ut nullum patiendi colligat usum
  neve relentescat saepe repulsus amor.
surda sit oranti tua ianua, laxa ferenti.
  audiat exclusi verba receptus amans.
et quasi laesa prior nonnumquam irascere laeso.
  vanescit culpa culpa repensa tua.
sed numquam dederis spatiosum tempus in iram.
  saepe simultates ira morata facit.
quin etiam discant oculi lacrimare coacti,
  et faciant udas illa vel illa genas.
nec si quem falles, tu periurare timeto;
  commodat in lusus numina surda Venus.
servus et ad partes sollers ancilla parentur
  qui doceant apte quid tibi possit emi,
et sibi pauca rogent; multos si pauca rogabunt,
  postmodo de stipula grandis acervus erit.
et soror et mater, nutrix quoque carpat amantem;
  fit cito per multas praeda petita manus.

Homer's great but the man who can give is greater.
Giving's a fine art, you know.

Never look down on an ex-slave with money.
What if his feet *were* coated with chalk?

And don't be fooled by family portraits. If a lover's broke
out he goes—and great-great-grandad with him.

Don't give a boy a free night because he's handsome—
tell him to raise the cash from one of his men-friends first.

Easy does it while you're setting the trap
but once he's caught squeeze him—hard as you like.

It does no harm to pretend you love him
provided you sell him the idea.

Don't always say yes: say you've a headache—
say you must go and worship Isis.

But don't overdo it. He may get used to feeling low
and his love cool off if you disappoint him too often.

Slam your door on serenades. Open it wide to presents.
Let lucky A hear B in the porch protesting.

You've wronged him? *You* are the injured party. Lose your temper.
Counter his grievance—he'll soon forget it.

But never be angry for long—
that only makes enemies.

And another thing: you must practise crying.
Specialise in tears of jealousy.

When you're deceiving him don't be afraid to swear you're not.
Venus never listens to lovers' lies.

You'll need a clever maid and a manservant to help
by telling him what gifts to get you.

They can ask for tips as well—
many a mickle makes a muckle.

Your mother and sister can cash in too—and your old nanny.
Many hands, quick money.

31

cum te deficient poscendi munera causae,
  natalem libo testificare tuum.

ne securus amet nullo rivale caveto;
  non bene, si tollas proelia, durat amor.

ille viri videat toto vestigia lecto
  factaque lascivis livida colla notis.

munera praecipue videat quae miserit alter.
  si dederit nemo, Sacra roganda Via est.

cum multa abstuleris, ut non tamen omnia donet,
  quod numquam reddas commodet ipsa roga.

lingua iuvet mentemque tegat. blandire noceque.
  impia sub dulci melle venena latent.

haec si praestiteris usu mihi cognita longo
  nec tulerint voces ventus et aura meas,

saepe mihi dices vivae bene, saepe rogabis
  ut mea defunctae molliter ossa cubent—'

vox erat in cursu cum me mea prodidit umbra.
  at nostrae vix se continuere manus

quin albam raramque comam lacrimosaque vino
  lumina rugosas distraherentque genas.

di tibi dent nullosque lares inopemque senectam
  et longas hiemes perpetuamque sitim.

ix

Militat omnis amans et habet sua castra Cupido—
  Attice, crede mihi, militat omnis amans.

quae bello est habilis Veneri quoque convenit aetas.
  turpe senex miles, turpe senilis amor.

quos petiere duces animos in milite forti,
  hos petit in socio bella puella viro.

If you're short of excuses for presents
wheel in the birthday cake.

Never let him take you for granted. Give him a rival.
Love thrives on competition.

Let him notice signs of another man in the bed
and a bruise or two on your neck.

Above all show him X's presents. If there aren't any
order them on appro—from the Via Sacra.

When he's given a lot vary your tactics and ask for a loan
which of course you'll never repay.

Be devious and chat him up. Sting as you kiss.
Honey hides the taste of poison.

In all my long experience I've never known these tips to fail.
So take my advice and don't be a scatter-brain.

Many's the time you'll bless me while I'm still alive
and pray my bones lie easy when I'm gone. . . .'

Her voice droned on but my shadow gave me away.
I was itching to get my hands

on that wispy white hair, those baggy cheeks
and bleary alcoholic eyes.

God give her nowhere to live, a penniless old age,
chronic winters, and an insatiable thirst!

ix

Yes, Atticus, take it from me—
lovers are all soldiers, in Cupid's private army.

Military age equals amatory age—
fighting and making love don't suit the old.

Commanders expect gallantry of their men—
and so do pretty girls.

pervigilant ambo. terra requiescit uterque.
    ille fores dominae servat, at ille ducis.

militis officium longa est via. mitte puellam,
    strenuus exempto fine sequetur amans.

ibit in adversos montes duplicataque nimbo
    flumina. congestas exteret ille nives.

nec freta pressurus tumidos causabitur Euros
    aptaque verrendis sidera quaeret aquis.

quis nisi vel miles vel amans et frigora noctis
    et denso mixtas perferet imbre nives?

mittitur infestos alter speculator in hostes,
    in rivale oculos alter ut hoste tenet.

ille graves urbes, hic durae limen amicae
    obsidet. hic portas frangit, at ille fores.

saepe soporatos invadere profuit hostes,
    caedere et armata vulgus inerme manu.

sic fera Threicii ceciderunt agmina Rhesi
    et dominum capti deseruistis equi.

nempe maritorum somnis utuntur amantes
    et sua sopitis hostibus arma movent.

custodum transire manus vigilumque catervas
    militis et miseri semper amantis opus.

Mars dubius nec certa Venus; victique resurgunt
    quosque neges umquam posse iacere cadunt.

ergo desidiam quicumque vocabat amorem
    desinat. ingenii est experientis amor.

ardet in abducta Briseide maestus Achilles—
    dum licet Argeas frangite, Troes, opes.

Hector ab Andromaches complexibus ibat ad arma
    et galeam capiti quae daret uxor erat.

summa ducum Atrides uisa Priameide fertur
    Maenadis effusis obstipuisse comis.

AMORES I ix 7–38

Lovers too keep watch, bivouac, mount guard—
at their mistress' door instead of H.Q.

They have their forced marches,
tramping miles for love,

crossing rivers, climbing mountains,
trudging through the snow.

Ordered abroad they brave the storm
and steer by winter stars.

Hardened to freezing nights,
to showers of hail and sleet,

they go out on patrol,
observe their rivals' movements,

lay siege to rebel mistresses
and batter down front doors.

Tacticians recommend the night attack,
use of the spearhead, catching the foe asleep.

These tactics wiped out Rhesus and his Thracians,
capturing the famous horses.

Lovers use them too—to exploit a sleeping husband,
thrusting hard while the enemy snores,

eluding guards and night patrols,
moving under cover.

If war's a gamble, love's a lottery. Both have ups and downs.
In both apparent heroes can collapse.

So think again if you think of love as a soft option—
it calls for enterprise and courage.

Achilles loved Briseis, sulked when he lost her—
Trojans, now's your chance to hammer the Greeks!

Andromache strapped Hector's helmet on
and sent him into battle with a kiss.

Great Agamemnon fell in love at first sight—
with Cassandra's wind-swept hair.

Mars quoque deprensus fabrilia vincula sensit.
notior in caelo fabula nulla fuit.

ipse ego segnis eram discinctaque in otia natus;
mollierant animos lectus et umbra meos.

impulit ignavum formosae cura puellae,
iussit et in castris aera merere suis.

inde vides agilem nocturnaque bella gerentem.
qui nolet fieri desidiosus amet.

X

Qualis ab Eurota Phrygiis avecta carinis
coniugibus belli causa duobus erat,

qualis erat Lede, quam plumis abditus albis
callidus in falsa lusit adulter ave,

qualis Amymone siccis erravit in Argis
cum premeret summi verticis urna comas,

talis eras; aquilamque in te taurumque timebam
et quicquid magno de Iove fecit amor.

nunc timor omnis abest animique resanuit error
nec facies oculos iam capit ista meos.

cur sim mutatus quaeris? quia munera poscis.
haec te non patitur causa placere mihi.

donec eras simplex, animum cum corpore amavi.
nunc mentis vitio laesa figura tua est.

et puer est et nudus Amor. sine sordibus annos
et nullas vestes, ut sit apertus, habet.

quid puerum Veneris pretio prostare iubetis?
quo pretium condat non habet ille sinum.

nec Venus apta feris Veneris nec filius armis.
non decet imbelles aera merere deos.

Even Mars was caught. Trapped in the blacksmith's net
he caused an epic scandal in the sky.

And what about me? I was soft—born in a dressing-gown.
A reading-couch in the shade had sapped my morale.

But a pretty girl soon put me on my feet—
Fall in she ordered, *follow me.*

And look at me now—alive and alert, the night-fighter.
Yes, if you want an active life try love.

X

You were my Helen, Ilion-bound from Sparta
to cause a war between two husbands,

my Leda, seduced by the white feathers
of a lecherous god,

my Amymone, lost in arid Argos,
balancing a pitcher on coiled hair,

and for your sake I was afraid of the eagle and the bull,
afraid of all Jove's amorous disguises.

But now, those fears are gone, my delusion cured.
Your face no longer haunts me.

Why am I changed? You keep asking for presents.
That's why I find you unattractive.

While you were straight with me I loved you body and soul,
but this inner twist disfigures the outer you.

Love is a naked child. His tender years
and the missing clothes are symbols of innocence.

Why ask the son of Venus to sell himself?
He wears no money-belt.

He and his mother hate aggression,
deserve better than mercenaries' pay.

stat meretrix certo cuivis mercabilis aere
    et miseras iusso corpore quaerit opes.

devovet imperium tamen haec lenonis avari
    et quod vos facitis sponte coacta facit.

sumite in exemplum pecudes ratione carentes.
    turpe erit ingenium mitius esse feris.

non equa munus equum, non taurum vacca poposcit,
    non aries placitam munere captat ovem.

sola viro mulier spoliis exultat ademptis,
    sola locat noctes, sola licenda venit

et vendit quod utrumque iuvat, quod uterque petebat,
    et pretium quanti gaudeat ipsa facit.

quae Venus ex aequo ventura est grata duobus,
    altera cur illam vendit et alter emit?

cur mihi sit damno, tibi sit lucrosa voluptas
    quam socio motu femina virque ferunt?

nec bene conducti vendunt periuria testes,
    nec bene selecti iudicis arca patet.

turpe reos empta miseros defendere lingua;
    quod faciat magnas turpe tribunal opes.

turpe tori reditu census augere paternos
    et faciem lucro prostituisse suam.

gratia pro rebus merito debetur inemptis;
    pro male conducto gratia nulla toro.

omnia conductor solvit mercede soluta;
    non manet officio debitor ille tuo.

parcite, formosae, pretium pro nocte pacisci.
    non habet eventus sordida praeda bonos.

non fuit armillas tanti pepigisse Sabinas
    ut premerent sacrae virginis arma caput.

e quibus exierat traiecit viscera ferro
    filius, et poenae causa monile fuit.

Even a prostitute, earning a bare living,
everybody's at a price, compliant,

curses the ponce she is forced to obey.
You are different—you can choose.

Learn from the animals—they don't calculate.
Brutes have kinder hearts than yours.

Do mares ask stallions for presents? Do cows ask bulls?
Do rams need presents to court their favourite ewes?

It's only women who love to plunder their lovers,
who hire out their nights and auction their bodies,

who sell shares in desire and joy
at a price that suits their selfish pleasure.

When love brings equal happiness to two people
why should either buy it from the other?

Why should sex, a co-operative venture,
be credited to your account and debited to mine?

If it's wrong for witnesses to be suborned,
for judges on the panel to accept bribes,

for defending counsel to be paid money,
for a court's proceedings to end in proceeds,

it's equally wrong to capitalize free love
and cash in on beauty.

Services rendered gratis rightly earn gratitude;
hired intercourse earns none.

Payment frees the customer from all commitment—
he owes you nothing for being obliging.

Beauty, beware. Think twice before taxing sex.
Greed can have nasty repercussions.

Settling for Sabine armlets Tarpeia
was crushed to death under Sabine arms.

In revenge for the bribe of a necklace
Alcmaeon murdered his own mother.

nec tamen indignum est a divite praemia posci.
　　munera poscenti quod dare possit habet.

carpite de plenis pendentes vitibus uvas.
　　praebeat Alcinoi poma benignus ager.

officium pauper numeret studiumque fidemque.
　　quod quis habet dominae conferat omne suae.

est quoque carminibus meritas celebrare puellas
　　dos mea; quam volui nota fit arte mea.

scindentur vestes, gemmae frangentur et aurum;
　　carmina quam tribuent fama perennis erit.

nec dare sed pretium posci dedignor et odi.
　　quod nego poscenti, desine velle, dabo.

xi

Colligere incertos et in ordine ponere crines
　　docta neque ancillas inter habenda Nape,

inque ministeriis furtivae cognita noctis
　　utilis et dandis ingeniosa notis,

saepe venire ad me dubitantem hortata Corinnam,
　　saepe laboranti fida reperta mihi,

accipe et ad dominam peraratas mane tabellas
　　perfer et obstantes sedula pelle moras.

nec silicum venae nec durum in pectore ferrum
　　nec tibi simplicitas ordine maior adest.

credibile est et te sensisse Cupidinis arcus.
　　in me militiae signa tuere tuae.

si quaeret quid agam, spe noctis vivere dices.
　　cetera fert blanda cera notata manu.

dum loquor hora fugit. vacuae bene redde tabellas.
　　verum continuo fac tamen illa legat.

However, it's not improper to ask the rich for presents—
they can well afford them.

Pick your grapes from prolific vines
and raid Alcinous' orchards

but let the poor man pay in kindness, loyalty, and love.
He can give his mistress all he has.

My special gift is verse, the praise of true beauty.
If I choose, my art can make you famous.

Dresses tear, jewels and golden trinkets break,
but poetic fame is a lasting present.

I'm ready to give but I hate your vulgar demands for payment.
Cut out demand and I'll supply.

xi

Napë, the coiffeuse,
no ordinary maid,

backstage-manager of my love-life,
my silent prompter,

keeper of Corinna's conscience,
averting crisis—

please, Napë, take her this note,
immediately.

You're flesh and blood,
no fool.

You must have suffered in Cupid's wars
so help a comrade in arms.

If she asks about me, say I live for our next meeting.
This note will explain.

But I'm wasting time. Hand it to her when she's free,
make sure she reads it then and there,

41

aspicias oculos mando frontemque legentis.
et tacito vultu scire futura licet.

nec mora, perlectis rescribat multa iubeto.
odi cum late splendida cera vacat.

comprimat ordinibus versus oculosque moretur
margine in extremo littera rasa meos.—

quid digitos opus est graphio lassare tenendo?
hoc habeat scriptum tota tabella—VENI.

non ego victrices lauro redimire tabellas
nec Veneris media ponere in aede morer.

subscribam VENERI FIDAS SIBI NASO MINISTRAS
DEDICAT. AT NVPER VILE FVISTIS ACER.

xii

Flete meos casus. tristes rediere tabellae.
infelix hodie littera posse negat.

omina sunt aliquid. modo cum discedere vellet,
ad limen digitos restitit icta Nape.

missa foras iterum limen transire memento
cautius atque alte sobria ferre pedem.

ite hinc difficiles, funebria ligna, tabellae,
tuque negaturis cera referta notis,

quam puto de longae collectam flore cicutae
melle sub infami Corsica misit apis.

at tamquam minio penitus medicata rubebas;
ille color vere sanguinolentus erat.

proiectae triviis iaceatis, inutile lignum,
vosque rotae frangat praetereuntis onus.

illum etiam qui vos ex arbore vertit in usum
convincam puras non habuisse manus.

and watch her face meanwhile—
there's prophecy in faces.

See she replies at once—a long letter.
Blank wax is a bore.

Get her to space the lines close and fill the margins
so it takes me longer to read.

Wait. Why tire her fingers pushing a stylus?
YES will do, in huge block capitals.

I'll garland those writing-tablets with Victory's laurel
and hang them up in the temple of Venus

above this dedication:
'From Naso—in wooden gratitude.'

xii

Weep for my failure—writing-tablets returned
with a sorry answer: *Can't manage today.*

The superstitious are right. Napë stubbed her toe
on the step as she left.

You must have been drinking, my girl.
Next time be more careful, and pick your feet up.

Damn these obstructive lumps of wood,
this wax frustration

obviously extracted
from Corsican hemlock honey,

coloured with cinnabar, I'm told,
but in fact—bloody.

The gutter's the place for this lumber
to be crunched under passing wheels.

I'm sure the man who made them
had felon's hands.

praebuit illa arbor misero suspendia collo,
    carnifici diras praebuit illa cruces.
illa dedit turpes raucis bubonibus umbras,
    volturis in ramis et strigis ova tulit.
his ego commisi nostros insanus amores
    molliaque ad dominam verba ferenda dedi?
aptius hae capiant vadimonia garrula cerae
    quas aliquis duro cognitor ore legat.
inter ephemeridas melius tabulasque iacerent
    in quibus absumptas fleret avarus opes.
ergo ego vos rebus duplices pro nomine sensi.
    auspicii numerus non erat ipse boni.
quid precer iratus nisi vos cariosa senectus
    rodat et immundo cera sit alba situ?

xiii

Iam super Oceanum venit a seniore marito
    flava pruinoso quae vehit axe diem.
quo properas, Aurora? mane: sic Memnonis umbris
    annua sollemni caede parentet avis.
nunc iuvat in teneris dominae iacuisse lacertis.
    si quando, lateri nunc bene iuncta meo est.
nunc etiam somni pingues et frigidus aer
    et liquidum tenui gutture cantat avis.
quo properas ingrata viris, ingrata puellis?
    roscida purpurea supprime lora manu.
ante tuos ortus melius sua sidera servat
    navita nec media nescius errat aqua.
te surgit quamvis lassus veniente viator
    et miles saevas aptat ad arma manus.

The tree they came from hanged a suicide—
supplied the executioner with crosses.

Horned owls hooted in its branches,
vultures and screech-owls brooded there.

I was mad to entrust these
with tender messages.

They were meant for deadly legal instruments
in the hands of some commissioner for oaths,

or to be wedged among a usurer's ledgers,
recording his bad debts.

Double-tablets? Double-crossers!
They say two's an unlucky number.

God rot their wood with worm
and their wax with white mildew!

xiii

Here she comes, over the sea from her poor old husband,
frosty axle turning, bringing the yellow day.

Why hurry, Aurora? Hold your horses, for Memnon's sake
and the annual sacrifice of his birds.

Now's the time when I love to lie in my love's soft arms,
the time of times to feel her body close to mine,

the time when sleep is heavy, the air cold,
and birdsong sweetest.

Why hurry? Lovers hate your company.
Tighten the reins in your rosy fingers.

Before your coming sailors can better watch their stars
and keep their course in open waters.

Travellers however tired rise when you appear
and soldiers reach for their weapons.

prima bidente vides oneratos arva colentes,
  prima vocas tardos sub iuga panda boves.

tu pueros somno fraudas tradisque magistris
  ut subeant tenerae verbera saeva manus.

atque eadem sponsum incautos ante Atria mittis
  unius ut verbi grandia damna ferant.

nec tu consulto nec tu iucunda diserto;
  cogitur ad lites surgere uterque novas.

tu, cum feminei possint cessare labores,
  lanificam revocas ad sua pensa manum.

omnia perpeterer, sed surgere mane puellas
  quis nisi cui non est ulla puella ferat?

optavi quotiens ne nox tibi cedere vellet,
  ne fugerent vultus sidera mota tuos!

optavi quotiens aut ventus frangeret axem
  aut caderet spissa nube retentus equus!

invida, quo properas? quod erat tibi filius ater
  materni fuerat pectoris ille color?

Tithono vellem de te narrare liceret:
  femina non caelo turpior ulla foret.

illum dum refugis longo quia grandior aevo,
  surgis ad invisas a sene mane rotas.

at si quem mavis Cephalum complexa teneres,
  clamares 'lente currite, noctis equi!'

cur ego plectar amans si vir tibi marcet ab annis?
  num me nupsisti conciliante seni?

aspice quot somnos iuveni donarit amato
  Luna, neque illius forma secunda tuae.

ipse deum genitor, ne te tam saepe videret,
  commisit noctes in sua vota duas.

iurgia finieram. scires audisse—rubebat.
  nec tamen adsueto tardius orta dies.

Your eye first lights on peasants shouldering their mattocks
and drags oxen under the yoke.

You rob children of sleep, condemn them
to classrooms and the cruel cane.

You send the unwary down to the Forum
to give their one-word promise and lose thousands.

Learned counsel deprecate your summons
to rise and shine again in court.

Back to the distaff and the daily stint
you call the housewife when her hands could idle.

I could stand all this, but pretty girls rising at dawn—
no lover can endure it.

If only night would defy you,
and the stars stare you out!

If only the wind would break your axle,
or frozen cloud give your team a fall!

Why hurry, spoil-sport?—Does Memnon's black skin
reflect the colour of his mother's heart?

I wish Tithonus could gossip about you—
he'd kill your heavenly reputation.

You run away from him because he's old—
he hates you getting up so early.

But if you slept with Cephalus, you'd shout
'Oh gallop slow, you midnight horses!'

I know your husband's senile, but why should my love suffer?
Did I arrange your marriage?

The Moon let her Endymion sleep for years—
and she's quite as beautiful as you are.

Even Jupiter couldn't stand the sight of you
that time he joined two nights of love together.—

My final thrust. She must have heard me—she turned pink.
But the sun came up on time—as usual.

xiv

Dicebam 'medicare tuos desiste capillos'.
  tingere quam possis iam tibi nulla coma est.

at si passa fores, quid erat spatiosius illis?
  contigerant imum qua patet usque latus.

quid quod erant tenues et quos ornare timeres,
  vela colorati qualia Seres habent,

vel pede quod gracili deducit aranea filum
  cum leve deserta sub trabe nectit opus?

nec tamen ater erat neque erat tamen aureus ille
  sed, quamvis neuter, mixtus uterque color,

qualem clivosae madidis in vallibus Idae
  ardua derepto cortice cedrus habet.

adde quod et dociles et centum flexibus apti
  et tibi nullius causa doloris erant.

non acus abrupit, non vallum pectinis illos.
  ornatrix tuto corpore semper erat.

ante meos saepe est oculos ornata nec umquam
  bracchia derepta saucia fecit acu.

saepe etiam nondum digestis mane capillis
  purpureo iacuit semisupina toro.

tum quoque erat neclecta decens, ut Thracia Bacche
  cum temere in viridi gramine lassa iacet.

cum graciles essent tamen et lanuginis instar,
  heu mala vexatae quanta tulere comae!

quam se praebuerunt ferro patienter et igni
  ut fieret torto nexilis orbe sinus!

clamabam 'scelus est istos, scelus, urere crines.
  sponte decent. capiti, ferrea, parce tuo.

xiv

I told you to stop using that rinse,
and now you've no hair left to tint.

Why couldn't you let it be? It grew in such profusion,
falling below your hips,

so fine one felt setting would spoil it—
like strands of Chinese silk

or the gossamer a spider spins
hanging from a high rafter.

It wasn't dark and it wasn't golden—
it was both and neither,

like the underbark of a tall cedar
in a green valley on Mount Ida.

Obedient too, easy to style and set,
it never made you lose your temper.

Grips and side-combs didn't break it.
Your maid could feel safe—

I've often watched her setting it
and you never jabbed a pin in her arm.

And I've often seen you before the morning ritual
lying back on your lilac couch

with ravelled hair—a Maenad tired of the dancing,
relaxed on a Thracian lawn. It suited you like that.

But delicate, and soft as down
what tortures it had to endure,

braving rack and ordeal by fire
to be twisted in tight spirals!

'It's a crime' I cried 'a downright crime to singe that hair.
It suits you as it is. Unsteel your heart.

vim procul hinc remove. non est qui debeat uri.
   erudit admotas ipse capillus acus.'

formosae periere comae, quas vellet Apollo,
   quas vellet capiti Bacchus inesse suo.

illis contulerim quas quondam nuda Dione
   pingitur umenti sustinuisse manu.

quid male dispositos quereris periisse capillos?
   quid speculum maesta ponis inepta manu?

non bene consuetis a te spectaris ocellis—
   ut placeas debes immemor esse tui.

non te cantatae laeserunt paelicis herbae,
   non anus Haemonia perfida lavit aqua,

nec tibi vis morbi nocuit (procul omen abesto!)
   nec minuit densas invida lingua comas.

facta manu culpaque tua dispendia sentis.
   ipsa dabas capiti mixta venena tuo.

nunc tibi captivos mittet Germania crines.
   tuta triumphatae munere gentis eris.

o quam saepe comas aliquo mirante rubebis
   et dices 'empta nunc ego merce probor.

nescioquam pro me laudat nunc iste Sygambram.
   fama tamen memini cum fuit ista mea.'

me miserum, lacrimas male continet oraque dextra
   protegit ingenuas picta rubore genas.

sustinet antiquos gremio spectatque capillos—
   ei mihi, non illo munera digna loco.

collige cum vultu mentem. reparabile damnum est.
   postmodo nativa conspiciere coma.

No violence, please. It's not for burning.
It can teach the tongs a trick or two.'

And now it's ruined—lovely hair
Apollo or Bacchus might have envied,

sleek as Dione's in the picture
where she rises naked from the waves.

You called it a mess and now you miss it. Silly girl,
don't put the mirror down so mournfully.

You must look at yourself with new eyes—
forget yourself if you want to be attractive.

It's not as if some rival had poisoned you
or a witch had washed you in unholy water.

You haven't been ill—touch wood—
and it wasn't the evil eye that thinned it.

You've only yourself to blame. You were asking for trouble
applying that concoction.

But thanks to our German triumph you're quite safe.
One of the women prisoners can send you hers.

The only trouble is when people admire it
you'll think 'I have to buy admiration now.

These compliments really belong to some Sygambrian girl.
Gone are the days when I deserved them.'

Poor dear, she's trying so hard not to cry,
shielding her face to hide the blushes,

staring down at the lost hair in her lap—
a keepsake regrettably misplaced.

Now put on your make-up and make up your mind the loss isn't final.
You'll soon be admired again—for home-grown hair.

XV

Quid mihi, Livor edax, ignavos obicis annos
    ingeniique vocas carmen inertis opus?

non me more patrum, dum strenua sustinet aetas,
    praemia militiae pulverulenta sequi!

nec me verbosas leges ediscere! nec me
    ingrato vocem prostituisse foro!

mortale est quod quaeris opus; mihi fama perennis
    quaeritur, in toto semper ut orbe canar.

vivet Maeonides Tenedos dum stabit et Ide,
    dum rapidas Simois in mare volvet aquas.

vivet et Ascraeus dum mustis uva tumebit,
    dum cadet incurva falce resecta Ceres.

Battiades semper toto cantabitur orbe—
    quamvis ingenio non valet, arte valet.

nulla Sophocleo veniet iactura cothurno.
    cum sole et luna semper Aratus erit.

dum fallax servus, durus pater, improba lena
    vivent et meretrix blanda, Menandros erit.

Ennius arte carens animosique Accius oris
    casurum nullo tempore nomen habent.

Varronem primamque ratem quae nesciet aetas
    aureaque Aesonio terga petita duci?

carmina sublimis tunc sunt peritura Lucreti
    exitio terras cum dabit una dies.

Tityrus et fruges Aeneiaque arma legentur
    Roma triumphati dum caput orbis erit.

donec erunt ignes arcusque Cupidinis arma,
    discentur numeri, culte Tibulle, tui.

Devouring Envy, why accuse *me* of wasting my life?
Why call poetry idlers' work?

The young shirker! What? Not following tradition?
Not earning a soldier's dusty decorations?

Not memorizing tedious laws or touting
rhetoric in the fickle Forum?

But your work dies. I want undying fame—
alive and singing, always, everywhere.

Homer's alive while Tenedos and Ida stand
and Simois runs to the sea.

Hesiod's alive while grapes fill with juice
and wheat falls to the sickle.

Callimachus the unoriginal master
will sing on—everywhere and always.

Can Sophocles come to a tragic end?
Aratus is safe as sun and moon.

While servants cheat and fathers storm,
while ponces grab and tarts flatter, Menander survives.

Blunt Ennius—impassioned Accius—
are names time cannot touch.

Shall Varro be forgotten? Argo on the slipway?
Jason's quest for gold?

Sublime Lucretius will endure
till the day when all the world dissolves.

Arms and the man, Farming and *Tityrus*
will be read while Rome is above the nations.

While Cupid's armed with torch and arrows
men will prize Tibullan grace.

Gallus et Hesperiis et Gallus notus Eois
    et sua cum Gallo nota Lycoris erit.

ergo cum silices, cum dens patientis aratri
    depereant aevo, carmina morte carent.

cedant carminibus reges regumque triumphi,
    cedat et auriferi ripa benigna Tagi.

vilia miretur vulgus: mihi flavus Apollo
    pocula Castalia plena ministret aqua,

sustineamque coma metuentem frigora myrtum
    atque ita sollicito multus amante legar.

pascitur in vivis Livor—post fata quiescit,
    cum suus ex merito quemque tuetur honos.

ergo etiam cum me supremus adederit ignis,
    vivam, parsque mei multa superstes erit.

Western lands and the lands of sunrise
will remember Gallus—and his Lycoris.

Time can destroy flints, and iron ploughshares,
but poetry is indestructible,

greater than kings and their triumphs,
rarer than Spanish gold.

The crowd go for tinsel. I choose golden Apollo,
a cup brim full of Castalian water,

a garland of sun-loving myrtle,
and my tormented audience—the lovers.

Envy feeds on the living but sleeps on tombs,
for each gets his due in the end.

Therefore beyond the last devouring flame
I too shall live—in the body of my work.

BOOK II

i

Hoc quoque composui, Paelignis natus aquosis,
 ille ego nequitiae Naso poeta meae.

hoc quoque iussit Amor. procul hinc, procul este, severi.
 non estis teneris apta theatra modis.

me legat in sponsi facie non frigida virgo
 et rudis ignoto tactus amore puer.

atque aliquis iuvenum quo nunc ego saucius arcu
 agnoscat flammae conscia signa suae,

miratusque diu 'quo' dicat 'ab indice doctus
 composuit casus iste poeta meos?'

ausus eram, memini, caelestia dicere bella
 centimanumque Gyen—et satis oris erat—

cum male se Tellus ulta est ingestaque Olympo
 ardua devexum Pelion Ossa tulit.

in manibus nimbos et cum Iove fulmen habebam
 quod bene pro caelo mitteret ille suo.

clausit amica fores: ego cum Iove fulmen omisi;
 excidit ingenio Iuppiter ipse meo.

Iuppiter, ignoscas: nil me tua tela iuvabant;
 clausa tuo maius ianua fulmen habet.

blanditias elegosque levis, mea tela, resumpsi:
 mollierunt duras lenia verba fores.

carmina sanguineae deducunt cornua lunae
 et revocant niveos solis euntis equos.

carmine dissiliunt abruptis faucibus angues
 inque suos fontes versa recurrit aqua.

carminibus cessere fores, insertaque posti,
 quamvis robur erat, carmine victa sera est.

AMORES II i 1–28

i

Another collection of verse by the man from Sulmona,
that embarrassingly personal poet Naso.

Another of Cupid's commissions. Hands off, moralists!
Love's tender strains will shock you.

I write for the girl who responds to her sweetheart,
and the boy in love for the first time.

I want every young man wounded like me by Cupid's bow
to recognize the symptoms of his fever

and ask himself in amazement 'How does this poet know
about me and my personal problems?'

Once, rashly, I sang of war in heaven and giants
with a hundred arms. My diction soared to the occasion—

the cruel vengeance of Mother Earth, and the piling
of Pelion upon Ossa upon Olympus.

But while I was busy with Jupiter standing on a storm-cloud,
thunderbolt at the ready to defend his heaven,

Corinna slammed her door. I dropped the thunderbolt
and even forgot the Almighty.

Forgive me, Lord. Your weapons couldn't help me.
That locked door had a far more effective bolt.

I returned to couplets and compliments, my own weapons,
and broke down its resistance with soft words.

The magic of verse can pull the blood-red moon out of orbit,
turn back the journeying sun's white steeds,

make rivers flow upstream,
split hooded snakes,

fling doors wide open, sliding
the strongest bolts from their staples.

quid mihi profuerit velox cantatus Achilles?
  quid pro me Atrides alter et alter agent?
quique tot errando quot bello perdidit annos?
  raptus et Haemoniis flebilis Hector equis?
at facie tenerae laudata saepe puellae,
  ad vatem pretium carminis ipsa venit.
magna datur merces. heroum clara valete
  nomina: non apta est gratia vestra mihi.
ad mea formosos vultus adhibete, puellae,
  carmina, purpureus quae mihi dictat Amor.

ii

Quem penes est dominam servandi cura, Bagoa,
  dum perago tecum pauca sed apta, vaca.
hesterna vidi spatiantem luce puellam
  illa quae Danai porticus agmen habet.
protinus, ut placuit, misi scriptoque rogavi;
  rescripsit trepida 'non licet' illa manu,
et cur non liceat quaerenti reddita causa est
  quod nimium dominae cura molesta tua est.
si sapis, o custos, odium, mihi crede, mereri
  desine; quem metuit quisque perisse cupit.
vir quoque non sapiens. quid enim servare laboret
  unde nihil, quamvis non tueare, perit?
sed gerat ille suo morem furiosus amori
  et castum multis quod placet esse putet;
huic furtiva tuo libertas munere detur,
  quam dederis illi reddat ut illa tibi.
conscius esse velis—domina est obnoxia servo.
  conscius esse times—dissimulare licet.

What good are epic heroes to me—the two Atridae,
Achilles fleet of foot,

Ulysses wasting twenty years in war and wanderings,
Hector dragged in the dust by Greek horses?

But sing the praises of a lovely girl
and she'll pay for the song in person.

A fair reward. Those famous names are out—
their gratitude means nothing to me.

My poems are written at Cupid's dictation
to catch the eye of Beauty.

ii

Can you spare me a moment, Bagoas? You chaperone this lady
and I'd like a few tactful words with you.

I saw her yesterday—strolling in the colonnade
among the statues of the Danaids.

She took my fancy. I wrote at once to ask for a meeting
and back came the timid answer *It's not allowed.*

On asking why, I learnt that you were the trouble—
you take your duties too seriously.

Be sensible about them and stop making enemies—
when we're afraid of someone we wish him dead.

Her husband's equally foolish. Why bother to guard
what loses nothing if unprotected?

Well, let him cultivate his amorous illusions
and think that what has many admirers can be chaste.

But present *her* with a gift—freedom to have affairs,
and she'll repay you with *your* freedom.

As confidant you'd have her in your power.
You think that's risky? Well then, turn a blind eye.

scripta leget secum—matrem misisse putato.
  venerit ignotus—postmodo notus erit.

ibit ad affectam quae non languebit amicam—
  visat, iudiciis aegra sit illa tuis.

si faciet tarde, ne te mora longa fatiget,
  imposita gremio stertere fronte potes.

nec tu linigeram fieri quid possit ad Isim
  quaesieris, nec tu curva theatra time.

conscius assiduos commissi tollet honores.
  quis minor est autem quam tacuisse labor?

ille placet versatque domum neque verbera sentit;
  ille potens, alii sordida turba iacent.

huic verae ut lateant causae finguntur inanes,
  atque ambo domini quod probat una probant.

cum bene vir traxit vultum rugasque coegit,
  quod voluit fieri blanda puella, facit.

sed tamen interdum tecum quoque iurgia nectat
  et simulet lacrimas carnificemque vocet.

tu contra obicies quae tuto diluat illa,
  et veris falso crimine deme fidem.

sic tibi semper honos, sic alta peculia crescent;
  haec fac—in exiguo tempore liber eris.

aspicis indicibus nexas per colla catenas?
  squalidus orba fide pectora carcer habet.

quaerit aquas in aquis et poma fugacia captat
  Tantalus—hoc illi garrula lingua dedit.

dum nimium servat custos Iunonius Io,
  ante suos annos occidit; illa dea est.

vidi ego compedibus liventia crura gerentem
  unde vir incestum scire coactus erat.

poena minor merito. nocuit mala lingua duobus:
  vir doluit, famae damna puella tulit.

AMORES II ii 19–50

If she's reading a note, assume it's from her mother
If a stranger turns up, let him get to know you.

If she wants to visit a girl-friend supposed to be ill,
accept the invalid story and let her go.

If she keeps you waiting, don't get impatient—
just relax, chin on chest, and snore.

And don't ask what goes on at the temple of Isis
or fear the worst in the crooked Theatre.—

But a confidant can always count on tips—
and is there an easier job than saying nothing?

He can do no wrong—upset the happy home and not get beaten.
He's the king-pin—the other servants mere dirt.

Your mistress can spin the yarns and hide the facts.
What satisfies her, will satisfy the master too.

Though husband frowns and scowls, in the last resort
he'll do as his little wife says.

But now and then she must make a point of scolding *you*.
When she calls you a callous brute and pretends to cry

you can tax her with something easily explained away,
so you won't be believed even when telling the truth.

Take my advice and you'll win respect—your savings will mount
and very soon you'll be buying your freedom.

Informers end up with chains round their necks—
you must have seen them. Traitors languish in jail.

Remember Tantalus in his pool, dying for a drink, clutching
at fruit just out of reach—because he couldn't keep his mouth shut;

and Argus, Io's over-conscientious guard,
who died suddenly—but she became a goddess.

I've seen a man with his legs festering in shackles
because he forced a husband to know the truth.

He deserved worse, for his malice did double damage—
broke a man's heart and ruined a woman's reputation.

crede mihi, nulli sunt crimina grata marito,
    nec quemquam, quamvis audiat, illa iuvant.

seu tepet, indicium securas perdis ad aures;
    sive amat, officio fit miser ille tuo.

culpa nec ex facili, quamvis manifesta, probatur;
    iudicis illa sui tuta favore venit.

viderit ipse licet, credet tamen ille neganti
    damnabitque oculos et sibi verba dabit.

aspiciat dominae lacrimas, plorabit et ipse,
    et dicet 'poenas garrulus iste dabit!'

quid dispar certamen inis? tibi verbera victo
    adsunt, in gremio iudicis illa sedet.

non scelus adgredimur, non ad miscenda coimus
    toxica, non stricto fulminat ense manus.

quaerimus ut tuto per te possimus amare.
    quid precibus nostris mollius esse potest?

iii

Ei mihi quod dominam nec vir nec femina servas,
    mutua nec Veneris gaudia nosse potes.

qui primus pueris genitalia membra recidit
    vulnera quae fecit debuit ipse pati.

mollis in obsequium facilisque rogantibus esses
    si tuus in quavis praetepuisset amor.

non tu natus equo, non fortibus utilis armis;
    bellica non dextrae convenit hasta tuae.

ista mares tractent, tu spes depone viriles;
    sunt tibi cum domina signa ferenda tua.

hanc imple meritis, huius tibi gratia prosit.
    si careas illa, quis tuus usus erit?

In fact no husband likes to hear tales about his wife.
They help no one, even if he listens.

If he's not in love, your evidence is wasted on him;
if he is, your sense of duty only makes him wretched.

Besides, unfaithfulness, even when blatant, is hard to prove.
The judge is prejudiced in his wife's favour.

If he's actually seen it, he'll still believe her flat denial,
condemn his own eyes and hoodwink himself.

She has only to burst into tears and he'll start sobbing too
and threatening to punish the tell-tale.

Why fight against odds? You're bound to be beaten, in both senses.
The accused is sitting pretty in her judge's lap.

We're not planning murder or coming together to brew poison.
I'm not flashing a drawn sword in front of you.

We're only asking your permission to make love.
Could any request be more considerate?

iii

Poor you! Neither male nor female, unable to share
the joys of sex, and yet keeping a mistress!

The man who first castrated boys
should have suffered the wound he inflicted.

I know you'd be sympathetic and obliging
if you'd ever felt the warmth of love.

But you weren't meant to ride or handle weapons;
you'd look unnatural gripping a spear.

Leave that to men. Renounce male ambition
and act as aide-de-camp to your mistress.

Serve her well and she'll reward you.
Where would you be without her?

est etiam facies, sunt apti lusibus anni.
  indigna est pigro forma perire situ.
fallere te potuit quamvis habeare molestus;
  non caret effectu quod voluere duo.
aptius at fuerit precibus temptasse; rogamus
  dum bene ponendi munera tempus habes.

iv

Non ego mendosos ausim defendere mores
  falsaque pro vitiis arma movere meis.
confiteor—si quid prodest delicta fateri.
  in mea nunc demens crimina fassus eo.
odi nec possum cupiens non esse quod odi.
  heu quam quae studeas ponere ferre grave est!
nam desunt vires ad me mihi iusque regendum.
  auferor, ut rapida concita puppis aqua.
non est certa meos quae forma invitet amores;
  centum sunt causae cur ego semper amem.
sive aliqua est oculos in se deiecta modestos,
  uror et insidiae sunt pudor ille meae.
sive procax aliqua est, capior quia rustica non est
  spemque dat in molli mobilis esse toro.
aspera si visa est rigidasque imitata Sabinas,
  velle sed ex alto dissimulare puto.
sive es docta, places raras dotata per artes;
  sive rudis, placita es simplicitate tua.
est quae Callimachi prae nostris rustica dicat
  carmina—cui placeo protinus ipsa placet;
est etiam quae me vatem et mea carmina culpet—
  culpantis cupiam sustinuisse femur.

She's in her prime, ripe for enjoyment;
such loveliness shouldn't be wasted.

For all your restrictions, she could have deceived you;
where there's a will there's a way.

But it seemed more tactful to try persuasion first
and give you the chance to make a good investment.

iv

I daren't excuse my weak character
by arguing falsely in self-defence.

I confess. They say confession helps.
Why not be reckless—conduct my own prosecution?

I hate what I am, but can't help wanting to be myself,
though it's hard to accept the unacceptable.

I lack the will-power for self-discipline—
get carried away—like a canoe over the rapids.

Beauty, for me, is not a monotype.
Incentives to love are legion.

Shyness, for instance, firing imagination
makes downcast eyes my downfall.

I admire the poise of a forward girl
and presume on her lively company in bed.

If she looks severe and unassailably virtuous,
I suspect she wants what she won't admit.

If she's cultured, her trained mind attracts me,
and if she's not, her naivety.

Then there's the fan who prefers me to Callimachus—
of course I become a fan of hers.

And the critic who carps at me and my work—
she needs a lesson in appreciation.

molliter incedit—motu capit; altera dura est—
    at poterit tacto mollior esse viro.

haec quia dulce canit flectitque facillima vocem,
    oscula cantanti rapta dedisse velim.

haec querulas habili percurrit pollice chordas—
    tam doctas quis non possit amare manus?

illa placet gestu numerosaque bracchia ducit
    et tenerum molli torquet ab arte latus—

ut taceam de me qui causa tangor ab omni,
    illic Hippolytum pone, Priapus erit.

tu, quia tam longa es, veteres heroidas aequas
    et potes in toto multa iacere toro;

haec habilis brevitate sua est—corrumpor utraque.
    conveniunt voto longa brevisque meo.

non est culta—subit quid cultae accedere possit;
    ornata est—dotes exhibet ipsa suas.

candida me capiet, capiet me flava puella,
    est etiam in fusco grata colore venus.

seu pendent nivea pulli cervice capilli,
    Leda fuit nigra conspicienda coma;

seu flavent, placuit croceis Aurora capillis.
    omnibus historiis se meus aptat amor.

me nova sollicitat, me tangit serior aetas;
    haec melior specie, moribus illa placet.

denique quas tota quisquam probat Vrbe puellas,
    noster in has omnis ambitiosus amor.

A graceful walk can step into my life.
Awkwardness requires male relaxation.

A silvery soprano tempts me
to steal a coloratura kiss.

If she plays the guitar *con amore*,
her fingers tug at my heart-strings.

The twining arms and swaying hips
of the cabaret dancer

could make Hippolytus priapic
let alone me.

The tall girl over there comes straight from Homer—
Andromache on a *chaise longue*.

Her friend's petite. I find both irresistible—
short or tall they measure up to my dreams.

I admire a girl in make-up for what she is
and a girl without for what she could be.

I love the pale and I love the golden
—the swarthy are lovely too.

Black hair on snow-white shoulders
reminds me of Leda's raven locks,

a platinum blonde of flaxen-haired Aurora.
Love, I find, mythologizes life.

I fall for the young and feel for the not so young—
one has the looks, the other the experience.

Put it like this—there's beauty in Rome to please all tastes
and mine are all-embracing.

V

Nullus amor tanti est—abeas, pharetrate Cupido!—
  ut mihi sint totiens maxima vota mori.

vota mori mea sunt cum te peccasse recordor,
  in mihi perpetuum nata puella malum.

non mihi deceptae nudant tua facta tabellae
  nec data furtive munera crimen habent.

o utinam arguerem sic ut non vincere possem!
  me miserum, quare tam bona causa mea est?

felix qui quod amat defendere fortiter audet,
  cui sua 'non feci' dicere amica potest!

ferreus est nimiumque suo favet ille dolori
  cui petitur victa palma cruenta rea.

ipse miser vidi, cum me dormire putares,
  sobrius apposito crimina vestra mero.

multa supercilio vidi vibrante loquentes.
  nutibus in vestris pars bona vocis erat.

non oculi tacuere tui conscriptaque vino
  mensa, nec in digitis littera nulla fuit.

sermonem agnovi quod non videatur agentem
  verbaque pro certis iussa valere notis.

iamque frequens ierat mensa conviva relicta,
  compositi iuvenes unus et alter erant:

improba tum vero iungentes oscula vidi—
  illa mihi lingua nexa fuisse liquet—

qualia non fratri tulerit germana severo,
  sed tulerit cupido mollis amica viro;

qualia credibile est non Phoebo ferre Dianam,
  sed Venerem Marti saepe tulisse suo.

V

Cupid, pack up your quiver. Is any love worth while
if it makes me long with all my heart for death?

And I long to die, my hell on earth, my darling,
when I think how you deceived me.

No secret notes, no presents smuggled in
laid bare your infidelity.

I only wish I couldn't prove it.
Why oh why is my case so good?

A man's in luck if his girl can say *Not Guilty*
and he can defend her with confidence.

It's callous and vindictive
to fight for a costly verdict against a sweetheart.

But I saw you both, with my own eyes. I was cold sober,
not, as you thought, asleep—though the wine was flowing.

I watched a conspiracy of eyebrows,
a confabulation of nods.

I could hear your eyes and decipher your fingers
and read the proposals you tabled in wine.

None of your innocent remarks escaped me—
the code was obvious.

When all the other guests had gone,
except a few young men, dead to the world,

I saw you kissing one another—
tongues deeply involved.

No sisterly kisses those,
but long and passionate—

the sort Venus gives Mars,
not Diana Phoebus.

71

'quid facis?' exclamo 'quo nunc mea gaudia defers?
   iniciam dominas in mea iura manus.

haec tibi sunt mecum, mihi sunt communia tecum.
   in bona cur quisquam tertius ista venit?'

haec ego quaeque dolor linguae dictavit. at illi
   conscia purpureus venit in ora pudor,

quale coloratum Tithoni coniuge caelum
   subrubet aut sponso visa puella novo;

quale rosae fulgent inter sua lilia mixtae
   aut, ubi cantatis, Luna, laborat equis,

aut quod, ne longis flavescere possit ab annis,
   Maeonis Assyrium femina tinxit ebur—

his erat aut alicui color ille simillimus horum,
   et numquam casu pulcrior illa fuit.

spectabat terram—terram spectare decebat.
   maesta erat in vultu—maesta decenter erat.

sicut erant—et erant culti—laniare capillos
   et fuit in teneras impetus ire genas.

ut faciem vidi, fortes cecidere lacerti;
   defensa est armis nostra puella suis.

qui modo saevus eram supplex ultroque rogavi
   oscula ne nobis deteriora daret.

risit et ex animo dedit optima, qualia possent
   excutere irato tela trisulca Iovi.

torqueor infelix ne tam bona senserit alter
   et volo non ex hac illa fuisse nota.

haec quoque quam docui multo meliora fuerunt
   et quiddam visa est addidicisse novi.

quod nimium placuere malum est, quod tota labellis
   lingua tua est nostris, nostra recepta tuis.

nec tamen hoc unum doleo. non oscula tantum
   iuncta queror—quamvis haec quoque iuncta queror.

'Stop' I shouted. 'That pleasure's mine.
I shall claim my rights.

You and I enjoy them in common.
Third parties are out.'

As I went on angrily speaking my mind
her face turned a guilty red—

red as the sky when Aurora paints it
or a girl first meeting her betrothed

red as a rose among pale lilies
or the harvest moon bewitched

or tinted Lydian ivory
that time never yellows.

Her blush was one of these, or maybe all.
She'd never looked more lovely—unintentionally.

She stared remorsefully at the ground—
remorseful staring suited her.

I felt like pulling her hair (it was perfectly set)
and scratching her eyes out

but when I saw her face my arms fell,
foiled by the feminine.

Anger vanished. I found myself begging
for kisses as good as those I'd watched.

She burst out laughing and treated me to her best—
they'd make an angry Jupiter drop his bolt.

Did the other man have my luck? The thought torments me.
I wish they'd been less good.

They were far better than the ones I taught her—
she must have had extra tuition.

It's a pity they gave me such pleasure,
a pity our tongues ever met,

because now I have two worries: kisses, yes,
but not only kisses.

illa nisi in lecto nusquam potuere doceri—
    nescioquis pretium grande magister habet.

vi

Psittacus, Eois imitatrix ales ab Indis,
    occidit. exsequias ite frequenter, aves.
ite, piae volucres, et plangite pectora pinnis
    et rigido teneras ungue notate genas.
horrida pro maestis lanietur pluma capillis;
    pro longa resonent carmina vestra tuba.
quod scelus Ismarii quereris, Philomela, tyranni,
    expleta est annis ista querela suis.
alitis in rarae miserum devertere funus;
    magna sed antiqua est causa doloris Itys.
omnes quae liquido libratis in aere cursus,
    tu tamen ante alios, turtur amice, dole.
plena fuit vobis omni concordia vita,
    et stetit ad finem longa tenaxque fides.
quod fuit Argolico iuvenis Phoceus Orestae,
    hoc tibi, dum licuit, psittace, turtur erat.
quid tamen ista fides, quid rari forma coloris,
    quid vox mutandis ingeniosa sonis,
quid iuvat, ut datus es, nostrae placuisse puellae?
    infelix, avium gloria, nempe iaces.
tu poteras fragiles pinnis hebetare zmaragdos,
    tincta gerens rubro punica rostra croco.
non fuit in terris vocum simulantior ales:
    reddebas blaeso tam bene verba sono.
raptus es Invidia. non tu fera bella movebas;
    garrulus et placidae pacis amator eras.

AMORES II v 61–vi 26

That sort must have been learnt in bed;
so at least one teacher has been well paid.

vi

Parrot is dead—the Indian mimic.
Flock, you birds, to his funeral.

Good birds all, with wings and talons
tear your hackles, beat your breasts.

Rend your feathers in lieu of hair,
in lieu of the trumpet flute your songs.

Ah Philomel, forget the crime of Tereus,
past centuries of lamentation.

Great loss was Itylus, but long ago—
transfer your tears to a rare contemporary.

All feathered aeronauts must weep for him,
especially his friend the turtledove.

They lived in full agreement,
faithful and true to the end,

Turtle the Pylades
to Parrot's brief Orestes.

But what avail devotion,
gorgeous colours, versatile voice,

Corinna's constant love? Alas
here lies Parrot, paragon of birds.

Greener his feathers than the brittle emerald,
his beak purple, with saffron spots.

Bird-master of impersonation
he was uniquely articulate.

But Fate, in envy, took him,
the prophet of non-violence

plenus eras minimo, nec prae sermonis amore
in multos poterant ora vacare cibos.

nux erat esca tibi, causaeque papavera somni,
pellebatque sitim simplicis umor aquae.

ecce, coturnices inter sua proelia vivunt,
forsitan et fiant inde frequenter anus.

vivit edax vultur, ducensque per aera gyros
miluus, et pluviae graculus auctor aquae.

vivit et armiferae cornix invisa Minervae,
illa quidem saeclis vix moritura novem.

occidit ille loquax, humanae vocis imago,
psittacus, extremo munus ab orbe datum.

optima prima fere manibus rapiuntur avaris;
implentur numeris deteriora suis.

tristia Phylacidae Thersites funera vidit,
iamque cinis vivis fratribus Hector erat.

quid referam timidae pro te pia vota puellae,
vota procelloso per mare rapta Noto?

septima lux venit, non exhibitura sequentem,
et stabat vacuo iam tibi Parca colo.

nec tamen ignavo stupuerunt verba palato;
clamavit moriens lingua 'Corinna, vale.'

colle sub Elysio nigra nemus ilice frondet,
udaque perpetuo gramine terra viret.

siqua fides dubiis, volucrum locus ille piarum
dicitur, obscenae quo prohibentur aves.

illic innocui late pascuntur olores
et vivax phoenix, unica semper avis.

explicat ipsa suas ales Iunonia pinnas;
oscula dat cupido blanda columba mari.

psittacus, has inter nemorali sede receptus,
convertit volucres in sua verba pias.

whose tastes were ascetic, whose love of talk
left little time for large meals.

Nuts were his diet, poppyseed his sleeping pills,
his drink plain water.

Aggressive quails reach riper years—
perhaps because their life is struggle.

Voracious vultures, circling kites,
rainmaker jackdaws, all live long.

Minerva's bugbear the carrion crow
can survive nine human generations.

But Parrot is dead, humanity's echo,
the talking gift from the Far East.

Fate always picks on the best first
and allows the worst to stay the course.

Thersites watched Protesilaus die,
and Hector was ashes long before his brothers.

I skip Corinna's anxious prayers—
a storm-wind blew them away.

On the seventh day, the day of doom,
Destiny stood with empty distaff.

But weak as he was he could still speak,
and his last words were *Goodbye, Corinna*.—

Under a hill in Elysium, a grove of black ilex grows,
and the ground is ever moist and green.

There, to the eye of faith, is the good birds' heaven,
barred to all birds of prey.

Harmless swans feed there at large
with the long-lived solitary phoenix.

Peacocks give spontaneous displays,
and amorous doves kiss and coo.

They have welcomed Parrot to a perch of honour
and applaud his pious ejaculations.

ossa tegit tumulus, tumulus pro corpore magnus,
　　quo lapis exiguus par sibi carmen habet:
COLLIGOR EX IPSO DOMINAE PLACVISSE SEPVLCRO.
ORA FVERE MIHI PLVS AVE DOCTA LOQVI.

vii

Ergo sufficiam reus in nova crimina semper?
　　ut vincam, totiens dimicuisse piget.
sive ego marmorei respexi summa theatri,
　　eligis e multis unde dolere velis;
candida seu tacito vidit me femina vultu,
　　in vultu tacitas arguis esse notas.
siquam laudavi, miseros petis ungue capillos;
　　si culpo, crimen dissimulare putas.
sive bonus color est, in te quoque frigidus esse,
　　seu malus, alterius dicor amore mori.
atque ego peccati vellem mihi conscius essem:
　　aequo animo poenam qui meruere ferunt.
nunc temere insimulas, credendoque omnia frustra
　　ipsa vetas iram pondus habere tuam.
aspice ut auritus miserandae sortis asellus
　　adsiduo domitus verbere lentus eat!
ecce novum crimen—sollers ornare Cypassis
　　obicitur dominae contemerasse torum.
di melius quam me, si sit peccasse libido,
　　sordida contemptae sortis amica iuvet!
quis Veneris famulae conubia liber inire
　　tergaque complecti verbere secta velit?
adde quod ornandis illa est operata capillis
　　et tibi per doctas grata ministra manus.

His bones lie decently buried, in a tomb as large as himself,
where a miniature headstone bears this brief inscription:

IN LOVING MEMORY OF POLLY,
A HIGHLY EDUCATED BIRD.

vii

So that's my role—the professional defendant?
I'm sick of standing trial—though I always win.

At the theatre I've only to glance at the back rows
and your jealous eye pin-points a rival.

A pretty girl need only look at me
and you're sure the look is a signal.

I compliment another woman—you grab my hair.
I criticize her—and you think I've something to hide.

If I'm looking well I don't love you.
If pale, I'm pining for someone else.

I wish to God I had been unfaithful—
the guilty can take their punishment.

As it is you accuse me blindly, believing anything.
It's your own fault your anger cuts no ice.

Remember the donkey, putting his long ears back—
the more he's beaten the slower he goes.

So that's the latest count against me—
I'm carrying on with your maid Cypassis?

Good God, if I wanted variety
is it likely I'd pick on a drudge like her?

What man of breeding would sleep with a slave
or embrace a body scarred by the lash?

Besides, she's your coiffeuse—her skill
makes her a favourite of yours.

scilicet ancillam quae tam tibi fida rogarem?
    quid, nisi ut indicio iuncta repulsa foret?
per Venerem iuro puerique volatilis arcus
    me non admissi criminis esse reum.

viii

Ponendis in mille modos perfecta capillis,
    comere sed solas digna, Cypassi, deas,
et mihi iucundo non rustica cognita furto,
    apta quidem dominae, sed magis apta mihi,
quis fuit inter nos sociati corporis index?
    sensit concubitus unde Corinna tuos?
num tamen erubui? num verbo lapsus in ullo
    furtivae Veneris conscia signa dedi?
quid quod in ancilla siquis delinquere possit,
    illum ego contendi mente carere bona?
Thessalus ancillae facie Briseidos arsit.
    serva Mycenaeo Phoebas amata duci.
nec sum ego Tantalide maior nec maior Achille.
    quod decuit reges cur mihi turpe putem?
ut tamen iratos in te defixit ocellos,
    vidi te totis erubuisse genis.
at quanto, si forte refers, praesentior ipse
    per Veneris feci numina magna fidem!—
tu, dea, tu iubeas animi periuria puri
    Carpathium tepidos per mare ferre Notos.—
pro quibus officiis pretium mihi dulce repende
    concubitus hodie, fusca Cypassi, tuos.
quid renuis fingisque novos ingrata timores?
    unum est e dominis emeruisse satis.

AMORES II vii 25–viii 24

I'd be mad to ask a maid so devoted to you.
She'd only turn me down and tell.

By Venus and Cupid's bow,
I'm innocent—I swear it!

viii

Cypassis, incomparable coiffeuse
who should start a *salon* on Olympus,

no country lass, as I know from our encounters,
but Corinna's treasure and my treasure-hunt—

who was it told her about *us*?
How does she know we slept together?

I didn't blush though, did I? Said nothing by mistake
to betray our secret?

I may have argued no one in his right mind
would have an affair with a maid,

but Achilles adored his maid Briseis
and Agememnon fell for his slave Cassandra.

I can't claim to be greater than those two.
What goes for royalty is good enough for me.

Corinna looked daggers at *you* though.
And how you blushed! I saw you.

But I saved the day, you must admit,
by swearing my Venus oath.

—Dear goddess, bid the warm south winds
blow that white lie over the ocean!—

So in return, my black beauty,
reward me today with your sweet self.

Why shake your head? The danger's over.
Don't be ungrateful. Remember your duty to *me*.

quod si stulta negas, index ante acta fatebor
    et veniam culpae proditor ipse meae,

quoque loco tecum fuerim quotiensque, Cypassi,
    narrabo dominae quotque quibusque modis.

ix

O numquam pro re satis indignande Cupido,
    o in corde meo desidiose puer,

quid me qui miles numquam tua signa reliqui
    laedis, et in castris vulneror ipse meis?

cur tua fax urit, figit tuus arcus amicos?
    gloria pugnantes vincere maior erat.

quid? non Haemonius, quem cuspide perculit, heros
    confossum medica postmodo iuvit ope?

venator sequitur fugientia, capta relinquit,
    semper et inventis ulteriora petit.

nos tua sentimus populus tibi deditus arma;
    pigra reluctanti cessat in hoste manus.

quid iuvat in nudis hamata retundere tela
    ossibus? ossa mihi nuda reliquit amor.

tot sine amore viri, tot sunt sine amore puellae—
    hinc tibi cum magna laude triumphus eat.

Roma nisi immensum vires promosset in orbem
    stramineis esset nunc quoque tecta casis.

fessus in acceptos miles deducitur agros,
    mittitur in saltus carcere liber equus,

longaque subductam celant navalia pinum,
    tutaque deposito poscitur ense rudis:

me quoque, qui totiens merui sub Amore, puella
    defunctum placide vivere tempus erat.

AMORES II viii 25–ix 24

If you're stupid enough to refuse I'll have to confess
and betray myself for betraying her.

I'll tell your mistress where and when we met, Cypassis,
and what we did and how many times and how we did it.

ix

Cupid, contempt's far more than you deserve
for loafing about in my heart.

Why pick on me? Have I ever deserted your colours?
Why am I wounded in my own camp?

Is it always friends your torch and arrows pierce and burn?
There'd be more glory in overcoming resistance.

Remember Achilles—who healed the wound
his spear gave Telephus.

No sportsman shoots at a sitting target—and after a kill
he presses on, following a fresh trail.

But opponents never feel your strength—it's we who suffer,
we the army of your faithful.

Thanks to you I'm little more than a skeleton—
why blunt the barbs of your arrows on bare bones?

There are so many looking for love, so many men and women
waiting for your day of glory.

Rome would still be a village of thatched huts
if she hadn't used her power to conquer the world.

The old soldier settles down on his small-holding,
the old race-horse enjoys the run of the woodland pasture,

ships of the line are laid up in dry dock,
gladiators exchange the sword for a harmless foil:

long service on love's active list has earned me my discharge
—it's high time I took life easy.

ixb

'Vive' deus 'posito' si quis mihi dicat 'amore',
    deprecer—usque adeo dulce puella malum est.

cum bene pertaesum est animoque relanguit ardor,
    nescioquo miserae turbine mentis agor.

ut rapit in praeceps dominum spumantia frustra
    frena retentantem durior oris equus,

ut subitus prope iam prensa tellure carinam
    tangentem portus ventus in alta rapit,

sic me saepe refert incerta Cupidinis aura
    notaque purpureus tela resumit Amor.

fige, puer. positis nudus tibi praebeor armis.
    hic tibi sunt vires, hic tua dextra facit,

huc tamquam iussae veniunt iam sponte sagittae—
    vix illis prae me nota pharetra sua est.

infelix tota quicumque quiescere nocte
    sustinet et somnos praemia magna vocat!

stulte, quid est somnus gelidae nisi mortis imago?
    longa quiescendi tempora fata dabunt.

me modo decipiant voces fallacis amicae—
    sperando certe gaudia magna feram—

et modo blanditias dicat, modo iurgia nectat,
    saepe fruar domina, saepe repulsus eam.

quod dubius Mars est, per te, privigne Cupido, est
    et movet exemplo vitricus arma tuo.

tu levis es multoque tuis ventosior alis
    gaudiaque ambigua dasque negasque fide.

si tamen exaudis pulchra cum matre rogantem,
    indeserta meo pectore regna gere,

ixb

Offered a sexless heaven I'd say *No thank you*—
women are such sweet hell.

Of course one gets bored, and passion cools, but always
desire begins to spiral again.

Like a horse bolting, with helpless rider
tugging at the reins,

or a gust catching a yacht about to tie up
and driving her out to sea,

Cupid's erratic air-stream hits me,
announcing love's target practice.

Then shoot, boy! I can't resist you.
Your aim strikes home in my heart.

Love's missiles lodge there automatically now—
they hardly know your quiver.

I pity the man whose idea of bliss
is eight hours' sleep.

Poor fool—what's sleep but death warmed up?
Resting in peace comes later.

Lead me astray, beguiling female voices.
Feed me on hope,

cooing today, cursing tomorrow,
locking me out and letting me in.

The fortunes of love. Cupid, Mars takes after you—
like stepson, like stepfather.

You're unpredictable, far more flighty than your wings,
giving delight, denying delight, evading question.

But maybe you and your lovely mother will hear this prayer:
be king of my heart for ever,

accedant regno, nimium vaga turba, puellae—
    ambobus populis sic venerandus eris.

X

Tu mihi, tu certe, memini, Graecine, negabas
    uno posse aliquem tempore amare duas.

per te ego decipior, per te deprensus inermis
    ecce duas uno tempore turpis amo.

utraque formosa est, operosae cultibus ambae,
    artibus in dubio est haec sit an illa prior.

pulchrior hac illa est, haec est quoque pulchrior illa,
    et magis haec nobis et magis illa placet.

erro, velut ventis discordibus acta phaselos,
    dividuumque tenent alter et alter amor.

quid geminas, Erycina, meos sine fine dolores?
    non erat in curas una puella satis?

quid folia arboribus, quid pleno sidera caelo,
    in freta collectas alta quid addis aquas?

sed tamen hoc melius quam si sine amore iacerem.
    hostibus eveniat vita severa meis.

hostibus eveniat viduo dormire cubili
    et medio laxe ponere membra toro.

at mihi saevus Amor somnos abrumpat inertes
    simque mei lecti non ego solus onus.

me mea disperdat nullo prohibente puella,
    si satis una potest—si minus una, duae.

sufficiam. graciles, non sunt sine viribus artus.
    pondere, non nervis, corpora nostra carent.

et lateri dabit in vires alimenta voluptas.
    decepta est opera nulla puella mea.

AMORES II ixb 29–x 26

let women, those floating voters, crowd into the kingdom
and both sexes join there in your worship.

X

Graecinus, I blame *you*. Yours that memorable remark
'No one can love two girls at once'.

I trusted you and dropped my guard. The result
is too embarrassing—a double love-life.

They're both beautiful, both sophisticated.
It's hard to say which has more to offer.

Certainly one is more attractive—but which one?
I love each more than either,

torn by a schizophrenic passion,
a catamaran in contrary winds.

Great Aphrodite, one girl's hell enough on earth—
why double-damn me?

Why add leaves to trees, stars to the Milky Way,
water to the deep blue sea?

Still, two loves are better than none at all.
God send my enemies a moral life,

single sleep and limbs relaxed
in mid-mattress.

But give *me* ruthless love—to interrupt my slumbers
with company in bed.

Let woman be my undoing—one, if one's enough—
otherwise two.

I can take it. I may be thin and under weight
but I've muscle and stamina.

Pleasure's a food that builds me up.
I've never disappointed a girl.

saepe ego lascive consumpsi tempora noctis,
  utilis et forti corpore mane fui.

felix quem Veneris certamina mutua perdunt!
  di faciant leti causa sit ista mei!

induat adversis contraria pectora telis
  miles et aeternum sanguine nomen emat.

quaerat avarus opes et quae lassarit arando
  aequora periuro naufragus ore bibat.

at mihi contingat Veneris languescere motu
  cum moriar, medium solvar et inter opus.

atque aliquis nostro lacrimans in funere dicat
  'conveniens vitae mors fuit ista tuae.'

xi

Prima malas docuit mirantibus aequoris undis
  Peliaco pinus vertice caesa vias,

quae concurrentis inter temeraria cautes
  conspicuam fulvo vellere vexit ovem.

o utinam ne quis remo freta longa moveret,
  Argo funestas pressa bibisset aquas!

ecce fugit notumque torum sociosque Penates
  fallacisque vias ire Corinna parat.

quid tibi, me miserum, Zephyros Eurosque timebo
  et gelidum Borean egelidumque Notum?

non illic urbes, non tu mirabere silvas;
  una est iniusti caerula forma maris.

nec medius tenuis conchas pictosque lapillos
  pontus habet—bibuli litoris illa mora est.

litora marmoreis pedibus signate, puellae—
  hactenus est tutum, cetera caeca via est—

Many's the night I've spent in love
and been fighting fit the morning after.

To die in love's duel—what final bliss!
It's the death I should choose.

Let soldiers impale their hearts on a pike
and pay down blood for glory.

Let seafaring merchants make their millions
till they and their lies are shipwrecked at last.

But when *I* die let me faint in the to and fro of love
and fade out at its climax.

I can just imagine the mourners' comment:
'Death was the consummation of his life.'

xi

Pines from the peak of Pelion started it—
Argo staggering the waves

in a reckless dash through the Clashing Rocks
to find and win the famous Fleece.

If only she'd sunk in those wild waters
and sea-going ships were unknown!

But now it's Corinna, leaving the shelter of home and bed
to go on a treacherous voyage.

Darling, why make me afraid of winds from east and west,
from icy north and spicy south?

Are there woodland walks or city splendours
in the cruel, blue, monotonous sea?

Delicate shells and coloured pebbles
are treasure-trove of the foreshore.

Beauty should walk the beach with shining feet;
beyond the water's edge lies danger.

et vobis alii ventorum proelia narrent,
　　quas Scylla infestet quasve Charybdis aquas,
et quibus emineant violenta Ceraunia saxis,
　　quo lateant Syrtes magna minorque sinu.
haec alii referant. at vos quod quisque loquetur
　　credite. credenti nulla procella nocet.
sero respicitur tellus ubi fune soluto
　　currit in immensum panda carina salum,
navita sollicitus cum ventos horret iniquos
　　et prope tam letum quam prope cernit aquam.
quod si concussas Triton exasperet undas,
　　quam tibi sit toto nullus in ore color!
tum generosa voces fecundae sidera Ledae
　　et 'felix' dicas 'quem sua terra tenet!'
tutius est fovisse torum, legisse libellos,
　　Threiciam digitis increpuisse lyram.
at si vana ferunt volucres mea dicta procellae,
　　aequa tamen puppi sit Galatea tuae.
vestrum crimen erit talis iactura puellae,
　　Nereidesque deae Nereidumque pater.
vade memor nostri, vento reditura secundo;
　　impleat illa tuos fortior aura sinus.
tum mare in haec magnus proclinet litora Nereus,
　　huc venti spectent, huc agat aestus aquas.
ipsa roges, Zephyri veniant in lintea soli.
　　ipsa tua moveas turgida vela manu.
primus ego aspiciam notam de litore puppim
　　et dicam 'nostros advehit illa deos!'
excipiamque umeris et multa sine ordine carpam
　　oscula. pro reditu victima vota cadet,
inque tori formam molles sternentur harenae
　　et cumulus mensae quilibet esse potest.

AMORES II xi 17–48

Let others tell you of tempests and tornadoes,
Charybdis' rock and Scylla's cave,

the stormy cliffs of Thunder Mountain,
the Libyan quicksands.

Believe what you hear. No storm can harm
a true believer.

Too late to look back when the rope's cast off
and your freighter heads for the far horizon,

when the captain scans the sky for squalls
and sees death as near as the water.

How pale you'll turn
if Triton sets the waves tossing!

How hard you'll pray to Leda's twins,
and how you'll envy people ashore!

It's far safer to put your feet up
and read a book or strum the guitar.

Still, if I'm wasting words on the winds
may Galatea do her level best for you.

On your heads be it, Nereids and father Nereus,
if such a girl is lost for ever.

Think of me, love, on the voyage out, and race home
with a stronger breeze filling the canvas,

wind and tide set fair for Italy,
Nereus tilting the sea this way.

Ask and the western airs shall blow.
Trim the sails with your own hands.

Down on the beach I'll be the first
to sight the ship that brings my idol.

I'll carry you ashore—smother you with kisses—
lay the promised victim low.

We'll make a couch of soft sand
with a dune for table

91

illic adposito narrabis multa Lyaeo,
    paene sit ut mediis obruta navis aquis,

dumque ad me properas neque iniquae tempora noctis
    nec te praecipites extimuisse Notos.

omnia pro veris credam, sint ficta licebit.
    cur ego non votis blandiar ipse meis?

haec mihi quam primum caelo nitidissimus alto
    Lucifer admisso tempora portet equo.

xii

Ite triumphales circum mea tempora laurus!
    vicimus. in nostro est ecce Corinna sinu,

quam vir, quam custos, quam ianua firma, tot hostes
    servabant ne qua posset ab arte capi.

haec est praecipuo victoria digna triumpho
    in qua, quaecumque est, sanguine praeda caret.

non humiles muri, non parvis oppida fossis
    cincta, sed est ductu capta puella meo.

Pergama cum caderent bello superata bilustri,
    ex tot in Atridis pars quota laudis erat?

at mea seposita est et ab omni milite dissors
    gloria, nec titulum muneris alter habet.

me duce ad hanc voti finem, me milite veni;
    ipse eques, ipse pedes, signifer ipse fui.

nec casum fortuna meis immiscuit actis;
    huc ades, o cura parte triumphe mea!

nec belli est nova causa mei. nisi rapta fuisset
    Tyndaris, Europae pax Asiaeque foret.

femina silvestris Lapithas populumque biformem
    turpiter adposito vertit in arma mero.

AMORES II xi 49–xii 20

and over the wine you'll spin me yarns
of giant waves that nearly drowned you,

of white squalls and black nights
and how you weren't afraid—because of me.

Invent it all, if you like. Your fiction shall be fact
and truth my heart's desire.

Oh bring me that day, bright Lucifer!
Bring it me soon—at full gallop.

xii

I wear the laurel; I have loved and won.
Corinna's here in my arms,

a prisoner freed from the Triple Alliance
of husband, chaperone, and door,

a prize of war, won without bloodshed,
ready for the Grand Victory Parade;

no mere defensive position with breastworks and a ditch,
but a live girl. There's leadership for you!

When Troy, besieged for a decade, fell at last,
it was little credit to Agamemnon.

But in this one-man operation
the kudos is all mine,

as commander and commanded,
as horse, and foot, and standard-bearer,

whose master plan eliminated luck
and achieved success by devotion to beauty.

Nor is the *casus belli* new:
two continents fought for Helen;

Centaurs and Lapiths brawled
at Hippodamia's wedding;

femina Troianos iterum nova bella movere
  impulit in regno, iuste Latine, tuo.
femina Romanis etiamnunc Vrbe recenti
  immisit soceros armaque saeva dedit.
vidi ego pro nivea pugnantes coniuge tauros;
  spectatrix animos ipsa iuvenca dabat.
me quoque, qui multos, sed me sine caede, Cupido
  iussit militiae signa movere suae.

xiii

Dum labefactat onus gravidi temeraria ventris,
  in dubio vitae lassa Corinna iacet.
illa quidem clam me tantum molita pericli
  ira digna mea, sed cadit ira metu.
sed tamen aut ex me conceperat aut ego credo;
  est mihi pro facto saepe quod esse potest.—
Isi, Paraetonium genialiaque arva Canopi
  quae colis et Memphin palmiferamque Pharon
quaque celer Nilus lato delapsus in alveo
  per septem portus in maris exit aquas,
per tua sistra precor, per Anubidis ora verendi
  (sic tua sacra pius semper Osiris amet
pigraque labatur circa donaria serpens
  et comes in pompa corniger Apis eat)
huc adhibe vultus et in una parce duobus,
  nam vitam dominae tu dabis, illa mihi.
saepe tibi sedit certis operata diebus
  qua tingit laurus Gallica turma tuas,
tuque laborantes utero miserata puellas
  quarum tarda latens corpora tendit onus,

Trojans waged war again
in Latium for Lavinia;

Sabines in Rome's infancy
fought to win back their women.

It's animal nature. I've seen two bulls battling for a heifer,
spurred on by her big brown eyes.

I am only one of Cupid's many campaigners,
bearing his standard, but avoiding bloodshed.

xiii

My foolish love, being pregnant, tried to end it
and now she lies at death's door.

How could she take that risk without telling me?
I ought to be angry but I'm only afraid.

Still, the child was mine, or at least I think so.
I'm apt to assume what's possible is fact.

O Isis, queen of Paraetonium and lush Canopus,
of Memphis and the palm-groves of Pharos,

and where the broad fast-flowing Nile
runs into the sea through seven mouths,

I beseech you by your sistrum, by Anubis' jackal head
(so may Osiris ever love your mysteries,

the sleepy snake slide round your treasure-chambers,
and the bull-god Apis follow your processions)

look down from heaven upon us and save two lives in one—
for hers depends on you and mine on her.

She has devoutly kept your days of supplication,
sitting where eunuch priests dip your sacred laurel,

and you are known to have compassion
on the heavy bodies of women in labour.

95

lenis ades precibusque meis fave, Ilithyia;
  digna est quam iubeas muneris esse tui.

ipse ego tura dabo fumosis candidus aris,
  ipse feram ante tuos munera vota pedes;

adiciam titulum *Servata Naso Corinna*,
  tu modo fac titulo muneribusque locum.—

si tamen in tanto fas est monuisse timore,
  hac tibi sit pugna dimicuisse satis.

xiv

Quid iuvat immunes belli cessare puellas
  nec fera peltatas agmina velle sequi,

si sine Marte suis patiuntur vulnera telis
  et caecas armant in sua fata manus?

quae prima instituit teneros convellere fetus
  militia fuerat digna perire sua.

scilicet ut careat rugarum crimine venter
  sternetur pugnae tristis harena tuae?

si mos antiquis placuisset matribus idem,
  gens hominum vitio deperitura fuit

quique iterum iaceret generis primordia nostri
  in vacuo lapides orbe parandus erat.

quis Priami fregisset opes si numen aquarum
  iusta recusasset pondera ferre Thetis?

Ilia si tumido geminos in ventre necasset,
  casurus dominae conditor Vrbis erat.

si Venus Aenean gravida temerasset in alvo,
  Caesaribus tellus orba futura fuit.

tu quoque, cum posses nasci formosa, perisses,
  temptasset quod tu si tua mater opus.

O Isis Ilithyia, hear my prayer, have mercy
and let her live, for she deserves your kindness.

And I shall wear white linen and burn incense on your altar
and lay my promised gifts at your feet,

recording thanks in stone for Corinna's safety
if only you will make it possible.—

This may be no time for advice, darling,
but never again risk your life in that mortal duel.

xiv

Why should girls be exempt from war-service
and refuse to follow the Amazons

if they carry lethal weapons in peace-time
and suffer self-inflicted wounds?

The first woman to tear an embryo from the womb
should have died of that assault herself.

How can you fight this duel on the sands of death
simply to save your stomach a few wrinkles?

If the mothers of old had followed your vicious example
mankind would be extinct—

we should need a second Deucalion
to renew our stony stock.

Who would have broken the power of Priam
had Thetis cut short her pregnancy?

Had Ilia murdered her unborn twins
who would have founded the queen of cities?

The world could wait in vain for Caesar
if Venus miscarried with Aeneas.

You yourself would have died unbeautiful
had your own mother been callous as you.

ipse ego, cum fuerim melius periturus amando,
    vidissem nullos matre necante dies.

quid plenam fraudas vitem crescentibus uvis
    pomaque crudeli vellis acerba manu?

sponte fluant matura sua. sine crescere nata.
    est pretium parvae non leve vita morae.

vestra quid effoditis subiectis viscera telis
    et nondum natis dira venena datis?

Colchida respersam puerorum sanguine culpant
    aque sua caesum matre queruntur Ityn.

utraque saeva parens, sed tristibus utraque causis
    iactura socii sanguinis ulta virum.

dicite quis Tereus, quis vos inritet Iason
    figere sollicita corpora vestra manu?

hoc neque in Armeniis tigres fecere latebris,
    perdere nec fetus ausa leaena suos.

at tenerae faciunt, sed non impune, puellae—
    saepe suos utero quae necat ipsa perit,

ipsa perit ferturque rogo resoluta capillos
    et clamant 'merito' qui modo cumque vident.

ista sed aetherias vanescant dicta per auras
    et sint ominibus pondera nulla meis.

di faciles peccasse semel concedite tuto
    et satis est—poenam culpa secunda ferat.

And is it not better for me to die of love
than be murdered by my mother?

Why rob the vine when the grapes are growing?
Why strip the tree of bitter fruit?

Let it ripen, ready to fall. Let first beginnings be.
New life is worth a little patience.

Why jab the needle in your own flesh
and poison the unborn?

We condemn Medea and Philomela
for murdering their children—

both were inhuman mothers: but both had bitter cause
to punish their men by such blood-sacrifice.

Is there a Jason or is there a Tereus driving you
to mutilate your own body?

No tigress in wild Armenia does that—
no lioness destroys her own cubs.

But tender-hearted girls do—and pay the penalty:
for the murderess often dies herself,

dies and is carried out in a shroud of hair to the burning,
and the people who see it shout *Serve her right!*

May my words vanish on the wind
and bring us no bad luck.

May the gods be gracious, overlook a first offence
and give her a second chance.

XV

Anule, formosae digitum vincture puellae,
  in quo censendum nil nisi dantis amor,
munus eas gratum. te laeta mente receptum
  protinus articulis induat illa suis.
tam bene convenias quam mecum convenit illi,
  et digitum iusto commodus orbe teras.
felix, a domina tractaberis, anule, nostra!
  invideo donis iam miser ipse meis.
o utinam fieri subito mea munera possem
  artibus Aeaeae Carpathiive senis!
tunc ego cum cupiam dominae tetigisse papillas
  et laevam tunicis inseruisse manum,
elabar digito quamvis angustus et haerens
  inque sinum mira laxus ab arte cadam.
idem ego, ut arcanas possim signare tabellas
  neve tenax ceram siccaque gemma trahat,
umida formosae tangam prius ora puellae—
  tantum ne signem scripta dolenda mihi.
si dabor ut condar loculis, exire negabo,
  adstringens digitos orbe minore tuos.
non ego dedecori tibi sum, mea vita, futurus
  quodve tener digitus ferre recuset onus.
me gere cum calidis perfundes imbribus artus
  damnaque sub gemmam perfer euntis aquae.
sed puto te nuda mea membra libidine surgent
  et peragam partes anulus ille viri.
inrita quid voveo? parvum proficiscere munus.
  illa datam tecum sentiat esse fidem.

XV

Signet-ring, tenant elect of a pretty girl's finger,
whose real value is the giver's love,

I wish you a warm welcome, and immediate installation
behind her second knuckle.

Fit her as snugly as she fits me,
gently hugging her finger.

Lucky you to be drawn on by my darling!
You make me jealous.

O for my metamorphosis into a ring,
by some desert island witch, or sea wizard!

Then, when I wanted to slip a hand inside her dress
and touch her breast,

I should squeeze my way off her finger
and drop by magic into her brassière.

Or suppose she was sealing a love-letter:
to stop the wax sticking to the stone

she'd kiss me first, with the tip of her tongue—
let's hope I shouldn't be sealing my own fate.

When she wanted to put me away, I'd refuse to move,
contracting, clinging tighter.

But I'd never embarrass you, darling,
or burden that delicate finger.

Wear me when you have a bath, and don't worry
if water seeps under the stone.

When you undress, I fancy my setting will rise
and I'll show you a phallic facet.

Fantastic thought.—Go to her, little gift,
and prove my love is genuine.

xvi

Pars me Sulmo tenet Paeligni tertia ruris,
  parva sed inriguis ora salubris aquis.

sol licet admoto tellurem sidere findat
  et micet Icarii stella proterva canis,

arva pererrantur Paeligna liquentibus undis
  et viret in tenero fertilis herba solo.

terra ferax Cereris multoque feracior uvae;
  dat quoque baciferam Pallada rarus ager,

perque resurgentes rivis labentibus herbas
  gramineus madidam caespes obumbrat humum.

at meus ignis abest. verbo peccavimus uno—
  quae movet ardores est procul, ardor adest.

non ego, si medius Polluce et Castore ponar,
  in caeli sine te parte fuisse velim.

solliciti iaceant terraque premantur iniqua
  in longas orbem qui secuere vias.

aut iuvenum comites iussissent ire puellas,
  si fuit in longas terra secanda vias.

tum mihi, si premerem ventosas horridus Alpes,
  dummodo cum domina, molle fuisset iter.

cum domina Libycas ausim perrumpere Syrtes
  et dare non aequis vela ferenda Notis.

non quae virgineo portenta sub inguine latrant
  nec timeam vestros, curva Malea, sinus,

nec quae submersis ratibus saturata Charybdis
  fundit et effusas ore receptat aquas.

quod si Neptuni ventosa potentia vincat
  et subventuros auferat unda deos,

Here I am at Sulmona, one of the Pelignian ridings,
small and fresh, a land of streams.

Even in the heat of July, when the parched earth cracks
and the Dog Star glitters,

there are clear waters winding through the Pelignian fields,
keeping them soft and green.

Wheat does well in this fine soil, the vine even better;
there are olive groves too

and deep meadow pastures, with loitering brooks
overhung by long grasses.

Still, my flame isn't here—or rather there's fire in my heart,
but the fire-raiser is far away.

Offered a place between Castor and Pollux,
I'd refuse heaven to be with her.

A troubled sleep in graves of clay
to the men who cut the world into roads.

If the world *had* to be cut up, they should have decreed
that lovers always travel together.

Then, as I tramped the wind-swept Alps,
my girl would make the going good.

With her I'd put to sea in a gale,
force my way through Libyan sandbanks,

laugh at the hell-hounds in Scylla's womb,
at the perils of Cape Malea,

and all the sunken wrecks
in Charybdis' whirlpool.

If Neptune's fury overwhelmed us,
sweeping away our guardian gods,

tu nostris niveos umeris impone lacertos—
    corpore nos facili dulce feremus onus.

saepe petens Heron iuvenis transnaverat undas;
    tum quoque transnasset, sed via caeca fuit.

at sine te, quamvis operosi vitibus agri
    me teneant, quamvis amnibus arva natent

et vocet in rivos currentem rusticus undam
    frigidaque arboreas mulceat aura comas,

non ego Paelignos videor celebrare salubres,
    non ego natalem, rura paterna, locum,

sed Scythiam Cilicasque feros viridesque Britannos
    quaeque Prometheo saxa cruore rubent.

ulmus amat vitem, vitis non deserit ulmum—
    separor a domina cur ego saepe mea?

at mihi te comitem iuraras usque futuram
    per me perque oculos, sidera nostra, tuos.

verba puellarum, foliis leviora caducis,
    inrita qua visum est ventus et unda ferunt.

si qua mei tamen est in te pia cura relicti,
    incipe pollicitis addere facta tuis,

parvaque quam primum rapientibus esseda mannis
    ipsa per admissas concute lora iubas.

at vos qua veniet tumidi subsidite montes,
    et faciles curvis vallibus este viae.

with her snow-white arms around me
I'd easily bear my lovely burden

remembering how Leander swam across to Hero,
safe, till the night her lamp was darkened.

But without you, darling, here among rows of vines
and brimming streams,

where the peasant sings as he opens the sluices
and a cool air rustles the olive leaves,

it's as though I'm not at Sulmona
on the farm where I was born,

but far away in Scythia, wild Cilicia, woad-painted Britain,
or perched on Prometheus' murderous crag.

Elm loves vine, vine clings to elm—
why are we two so often parted?

You promised never to leave me, swore it on my life
by those twin stars your eyes.

But a woman's word is lighter than a leaf falling,
floating away on the wind or the water.

If in your heart you pity my loneliness,
don't promise—act.

Harness the Gallic ponies and race here in the trap,
cracking the whip over their flying manes,

and the roads in the winding valleys will straighten out for you,
and the high mountains level down as you pass.

105

xvii

Siquis erit qui turpe putet servire puellae,
    illo convincar iudice turpis ego.

sim licet infamis, dum me moderatius urat
    quae Paphon et fluctu pulsa Cythera tenet.

atque utinam dominae miti quoque praeda fuissem,
    formosae quoniam praeda futurus eram.

dat facies animos. facie violenta Corinna est.
    me miserum, cur est tam bene nota sibi?

scilicet a speculi sumuntur imagine fastus,
    nec nisi compositam se prius illa videt.

non, tibi si facies nimium dat in omnia regni—
    o facies oculos nata tenere meos!—

collatum idcirco tibi me contemnere debes.
    aptari magnis inferiora licet.

traditur et nymphe mortalis amore Calypso
    capta recusantem detinuisse virum.

creditur aequoream Pthio Nereida regi,
    Egeriam iusto concubuisse Numae.

Volcani Venus est, quamvis incude relicta
    turpiter obliquo claudicet ille pede.

carminis hoc ipsum genus impar, sed tamen apte
    iungitur herous cum breviore modo.

tu quoque me, mea lux, in quaslibet accipe leges;
    te deceat medio iura dedisse toro.

non tibi crimen ero nec quo laetere remoto.
    non erit hic nobis infitiandus amor.

sunt mihi pro magno felicia carmina censu,
    et multae per me nomen habere volunt.

xvii

It's immoral, you say, to be a woman's slave?
All right then—label me an immoralist.

I'd welcome disgrace if only the island goddess
would show me cool consideration.

If I was fated to fall for beauty
couldn't my beautiful fate be kind?

But beauty is proud—beauty makes Corinna hard.
Alas she knows herself too well,

prides herself on daily reflexion,
the blinkered study of her make-up.

O beauty, born to hold my gaze,
although you reign in Beauty's right

you wrong me by disdain.
Can't greatness condescend?

Calypso fell in mortal love—
kept a reluctant man.

Peleus slept with a Nereid,
Numa with a Naiad.

Vulcan limps from his anvil
home to bed with Venus.

These two lines are odd
but five and six make one.

So take me, love—on any terms.
Rule me from the bed of justice.

I shan't disgrace you, and you'd miss me.
We never need disown our love.

My capital is balanced couplets.
Women apply to me for credit.

novi aliquam quae se circumferat esse Corinnam.
  ut fiat quid non illa dedisse velit?
sed neque diversi ripa labuntur eadem
  frigidus Eurotas populiferque Padus,
nec nisi tu nostris cantabitur ulla libellis—
  ingenio causas tu dabis una meo.

xviii

Carmen ad iratum dum tu perducis Achillem
  primaque iuratis induis arma viris,
nos, Macer, ignava Veneris cessamus in umbra
  et tener ausuros grandia frangit Amor.
saepe meae 'tandem' dixi 'discede' puellae—
  in gremio sedit protinus illa meo.
saepe 'pudet' dixi—lacrimis vix illa retentis
  'me miseram iam te' dixit 'amare pudet?'
implicuitque suos circum mea colla lacertos
  et quae me perdunt oscula mille dedit.
vincor et ingenium sumptis revocatur ab armis
  resque domi gestas et mea bella cano.
sceptra tamen sumpsi curaque tragoedia nostra
  crevit et huic operi quamlibet aptus eram:
risit Amor pallamque meam pictosque cothurnos
  sceptraque privata tam cito sumpta manu;
hinc quoque me dominae numen deduxit iniquae
  deque cothurnato vate triumphat Amor.
quod licet, aut artes teneri profitemur amoris—
  ei mihi, praeceptis urgeor ipse meis!—
aut quod Penelopes verbis reddatur Vlixi
  scribimus et lacrimas, Phylli relicta, tuas,

I know your would-be namesake—
she'd pay me to be you.

But Padus and Eurotas
run separate ways for ever,

and I shall always be *your* poet,
and you alone my theme.

xviii

While you continue your epic advance on Achilles' wrath
and arm the heroes who swore to revenge Menelaus,

I am defaulting, Macer, in the shady walks of love,
where Cupid shatters my high-poetic hopes.

I keep telling my girl it's all over between us
and next moment find her in my lap.

I say I'm ashamed of myself and she retorts in tears
'But not, surely, of loving little me?'

Then she flings her arms round my neck and gives me
a thousand demoralizing kisses.

That finishes me. Seconded from the field of epic
I report on the home front and war between the sexes.

Lately, though, I grasped the sceptre and wrote a tragedy,
finding the genre suited my genius,

but Cupid laughed at my royal robes and red leather boots
and the sceptre I'd usurped so rashly,

and once again I bowed to the will of a jealous woman—
Love triumphant over the tragic bard.

So now I do what I can—lecture in verse on the art of love,
exposing myself to attack by my own pupils—

or write love-letters—Penelope to Ulysses,
a *cri de cœur* from deserted Phyllis,

quod Paris et Macareus et quod male gratus Iason
    Hippolytique parens Hippolytusque legant,

quodque tenens strictum Dido miserabilis ensem
    dicat et Aeoliam Lesbis amica lyram.

quam cito de toto rediit meus orbe Sabinus
    scriptaque diversis rettulit ipse locis!

candida Penelope signum cognovit Vlixis,
    legit ab Hippolyto scripta noverca suo;

iam pius Aeneas miserae rescripsit Elissae,
    quodque legat Phyllis, si modo vivit, adest;

tristis ad Hypsipylen ab Iasone littera venit,
    dat votam Phoebo Lesbis amata lyram.

nec tibi, qua tutum vati, Macer, arma canenti,
    aureus in medio Marte tacetur Amor:

et Paris est illic et adultera, nobile crimen,
    et comes extincto Laodamia viro.

si bene te novi, non bella libentius istis
    dicis, et a vestris in mea castra venis.

xix

Si tibi non opus est servata, stulte, puella,
    at mihi fac serves quo magis ipse velim.

quod licet ingratum est; quod non licet acrius urit.
    ferreus est si quis quod sinit alter amat.

speremus pariter, pariter metuamus amantes,
    et faciat voto rara repulsa locum.

quo mihi formosam quae numquam fallere curet?
    nil ego quod nullo tempore laedat amo.

viderat hoc in me vitium versuta Corinna
    quaque capi possem callida norat opem.

mail for ungrateful Jason, for Macareus and Paris,
for Theseus and his son Hippolytus,

a monologue from poor Dido holding a sword,
another from Sappho holding her Lesbian lyre.

How quickly my friend Sabinus returned from his world-tour
and brought back replies from distant addresses!

Penelope can recognize Ulysses' writing;
Phaedra reads a note from her stepson;

Aeneas, dutiful once more, replies to unhappy Dido,
and Phyllis, were she alive, could hear from Demophoon;

a cruel letter from Jason reaches Hypsipyle;
Sappho feels loved and presents her lyre to Phoebus.

Even you, dear Macer, saving your epic dignity,
sing of golden love in wartime,

of Paris and Helen, faithless but world-famous,
of Laodamia, faithful unto death.

I'm sure these suit your book far better than battles.
You'll soon be posted as an epic deserter.

xix

Guard your girl, stupid—if only to please *me*.
I want to want her more.

I'm bored by what's allowed, what isn't fascinates me.
Love by another man's leave is too cold-blooded.

Lovers need a co-existence of hope and fear—
a few disappointments help us to dream.

I write off beautiful women who won't bother to deceive me.
I can't love what never turns nasty.

Corinna, clever girl, noticed this weakness of mine
and knew the best way to exploit it.

a quotiens sani capitis mentita dolores
   cunctantem tardo iussit abire pede!

a quotiens finxit culpam, quantumque licebat
   insonti, speciem praebuit esse nocens!

sic ubi vexarat tepidosque refoverat ignis,
   rursus erat votis comis et apta meis.

quas mihi blanditias, quam dulcia verba parabat!
   oscula, di magni, qualia quotque dabat!

tu quoque quae nostros rapuisti nuper ocellos
   saepe time insidias, saepe rogata nega,

et sine me ante tuos proiectum in limine postis
   longa pruinosa frigora nocte pati.

sic mihi durat amor longosque adolescit in annos;
   hoc iuvat, haec animi sunt alimenta mei.

pinguis amor nimiumque patens in taedia nobis
   vertitur et stomacho dulcis ut esca nocet.

si numquam Danaen habuisset aenea turris,
   non esset Danae de Iove facta parens.

dum servat Iuno mutatam cornibus Io,
   facta est quam fuerat gratior illa Iovi.

quod licet et facile est quisquis cupit arbore frondes
   carpat et e magno flumine potet aquam.

si qua volet regnare diu, deludat amantem—
   ei mihi, ne monitis torquear ipse meis!

quidlibet eveniat, nocet indulgentia nobis;
   quod sequitur fugio, quod fugit ipse sequor.

at tu, formosae nimium secure puellae,
   incipe iam prima claudere nocte forem,

incipe quis totiens furtim tua limina pulset
   quaerere, quid latrent nocte silente canes,

quas ferat et referat sollers ancilla tabellas,
   cur totiens vacuo secubet ipsa toro.

Sometimes she'd invent a head-ache
and tell me to clear off,

sometimes she'd say she'd been unfaithful
and look as if she really had.

Then, having fanned my fading passion to a blaze,
she'd be sweet again and exquisitely obliging.

What irresistible temptation she could offer,
and oh my God the artistry of her kisses!

You too, latest and dearest, must learn to look alarmed
and master the art of saying No.

Let me lie full length on your doorstep
all frosty night long,

and my love will last, growing stronger as time passes—
that's the way to keep passion in training.

Love on a plate soon palls—
like eating too much cake.

Danae unconfined
would have missed her famous confinement.

Io as a heifer
doubled her human charm.

If you want what's easy to get pick leaves off trees,
drink Tiber water,

but if you want your power to last deceive your lover.
Perhaps I'll live to regret that advice,

but come what may it's cruel to be too kind.
If you want to be chased you must run away.

As for you, sir, Beauty's blissful ignoramus,
start locking up at nightfall,

ask about those taps on the door,
the dogs barking in the small hours,

all those notes the maid delivers,
and why the mistress wants to sleep alone.

mordeat ista tuas aliquando cura medullas
    daque locum nostris materiamque dolis.

ille potest vacuo furari litore harenas
    uxorem stulti si quis amare potest.

iamque ego praemoneo: nisi tu servare puellam
    incipis, incipiet desinere esse mea.

multa diuque tuli, speravi saepe futurum,
    cum bene servasses, ut bene verba darem;

lentus es et pateris nulli patienda marito.
    at mihi concessa finis amoris erit.

scilicet infelix numquam prohibebor adire?
    nox mihi sub nullo vindice semper erit?

nil metuam? per nulla traham suspiria somnos?
    nil facies cur te iure perisse velim?

quid mihi cum facili, quid cum lenone marito?
    corrumpit vitio gaudia nostra suo.

quin alium quem tanta iuvet patientia quaeris?
    me tibi rivalem si iuvat esse, veta.

Become concerned. Allow suspicion to prey on you
and give me a chance to show my skill.

An affair with the wife of a fool
is stealing sand from the beach.

I'm warning you: start guarding your girl
or I'll stop wanting her.

I've suffered long enough—in the vain hope
you'd take precautions so I could take advantage.

But you won't react like a normal husband
and I can't make love on sufferance.

Shall I never be locked out
or face reprisals one fine night?

Never be scared? Never insomniac or sad?
Can't you give me some excuse for wishing you dead?

I don't approve of uncomplaining, pimping husbands—
their immorality ruins my pleasure.

Find someone who can appreciate your perversion,
or, if you value *me* as a rival, use your veto.

BOOK III

i

Stat vetus et multos incaedua silva per annos;
    credibile est illi numen inesse loco.

fons sacer in medio speluncaque pumice pendens,
    et latere ex omni dulce queruntur aves.

hic ego dum spatior tectus nemoralibus umbris—
    quod mea quaerebam Musa moveret opus—

venit odoratos Elegia nexa capillos,
    et puto pes illi longior alter erat.

forma decens, vestis tenuissima, vultus amantis,
    et pedibus vitium causa decoris erat.

venit et ingenti violenta Tragoedia passu;
    fronte comae torva, palla iacebat humi,

laeva manus sceptrum late regale movebat,
    Lydius alta pedum vincla cothurnus erat.

et prior 'ecquis erit' dixit 'tibi finis amandi,
    o argumenti lente poeta tui?

nequitiam vinosa tuam convivia narrant,
    narrant in multas compita secta vias.

saepe aliquis digito vatem designat euntem
    atque ait "hic, hic est quem ferus urit Amor."

fabula, nec sentis, tota iactaris in Vrbe
    dum tua praeterito facta pudore refers.

tempus erat thyrso pulsum graviore moveri.
    cessatum satis est. incipe maius opus.

materia premis ingenium. cane facta virorum—
    "haec animo" dices "area digna meo est."

quod tenerae cantent lusit tua Musa puellae,
    primaque per numeros acta iuventa suos.

i

An ancient wood, for many years unlopped by the axe,
haunted, one felt, by an unseen presence.

In the middle a cave, arching over a sacred spring,
and everywhere the plaintive singing of birds.

I was strolling here, in leafy twilight,
wondering what my next poem should be,

when Elegy appeared, her perfumed hair swept-up,
and one foot shorter, I think, than the other.

The fault was oddly attractive. She had style,
an elegant ensemble, a loving look.

Tragedy followed, a stormy figure, striding along,
hair over furrowed brow, mantle trailing,

wearing high Lydian boots and holding a sceptre
imperiously in her left hand.

'Poet' she exclaimed 'haven't you finished with love yet?
Aren't you tired of that tiresome subject?

Your escapades are the talk of every drunken party
and every back-street corner.

People stare and point at you as you walk past—
"That's him" they say, "there's goes Cupid's firework."

Those indecent exposés of your private life
have made you a Roman scandal—and you can't see it.

It's time you felt the full weight of Bacchus' rod.
Stop shirking. Start a major work.

Your talent needs more scope: great men and their achievements—
that, you'll find, is your proper field.

So far you've thrown off some pretty lyrics for the girls,
but the time for juvenilia is over.

nunc habeam per te Romana Tragoedia nomen;
  implebit leges spiritus iste meas.'
hactenus, et movit pictis innixa cothurnis
  densum caesarie terque quaterque caput.
altera, si memini, limis subrisit ocellis.
  fallor an in dextra myrtea virga fuit?
'quid gravibus verbis, animosa Tragoedia,' dixit
  'me premis? an numquam non gravis esse potes?
imparibus tamen es numeris dignata moveri;
  in me pugnasti versibus usa meis.
non ego contulerim sublimia carmina nostris;
  obruit exiguas regia vestra fores.
sum levis, et mecum levis est mea cura Cupido.
  non sum materia fortior ipsa mea.
rustica sit sine me lascivi mater Amoris;
  huic ego proveni lena comesque deae.
quam tu non poteris duro reserare cothurno,
  haec est blanditiis ianua laxa meis.
per me decepto didicit custode Corinna
  liminis adstricti sollicitare fidem,
delabique toro tunica velata soluta
  atque impercussos nocte movere pedes.
et tamen emerui plus quam tu posse ferendo
  multa supercilio non patienda tuo.
vel quotiens foribus duris infixa pependi,
  non verita a populo praetereunte legi!
quin ego me memini, dum custos saevus abiret,
  ancillae miseram delituisse sinu.
quid cum me munus natali mittis, at illa
  rumpit et adposita barbara mergit aqua?
prima tuae movi felicia semina mentis.
  munus habes, quod te iam petit ista, meum.'

Roman Tragedy waits for you to make her famous—
for your vitality to satisfy her needs.'

At this, bolt upright in those high red boots,
she nodded four times, tossing her thick hair.

Elegy—armed, I think, with a myrtle wand—
smiled at her maliciously.

'Pompous creature!' she said. 'You and your moralizing!
Can't you ever be light-hearted?

Thank you for condescending to preach in couplets—
for attacking me in my own metre.

I have no wish to aspire to your sublime.
Your palace dwarfs my little door.

I'm gay and frivolous, like my darling Cupid—
as unheroic as my theme.

But without me Venus would be vulgar—
she needs me as mentor and manager.

The door your high boot can't kick open
opens wide to my sweet words.

I taught Corinna to trick her escort
and tamper with trusty locks,

to slip out of bed in her nightdress
and tiptoe through the dark.

My power is greater than yours because I've suffered—
things your pride could never endure.

Many's the time I've been pinned against a locked door
and braved the stares of passers-by.

What's more I remember hiding in a maid's dress
till the chaperone was out of the way.

I've even been torn apart and plunged in water
when I went as birthday present to that illiterate girl.

It was I awakened your poetic gift;
it's thanks to me this woman is after you now.'

desierat. coepi 'per vos utramque rogamus
  in vacuas aures verba timentis eant.

altera me sceptro decoras altoque cothurno.
  iam nunc contacto magnus in ore sonus.

altera das nostro victurum nomen amori.
  ergo ades et longis versibus adde breves.

exiguum vati concede, Tragoedia, tempus.
  tu labor aeternus. quod petit illa breve est.'

mota dedit veniam. teneri properentur Amores
  dum vacat. a tergo grandius urget opus.

ii

'Non ego nobilium sedeo studiosus equorum—
  cui tamen ipsa faves, vincat ut ille precor.

ut loquerer tecum veni tecumque sederem,
  ne tibi non notus quem facis esset amor.

tu cursus spectas, ego te. spectemus uterque
  quod iuvat, atque oculos pascat uterque suos.

o cuicumque faves felix agitator equorum!
  ergo illi curae contigit esse tuae?

hoc mihi contingat, sacro de carcere missis
  insistam forti mente vehendus equis,

et modo lora dabo, modo verbere terga notabo,
  nunc stringam metas interiore rota.

si mihi currenti fueris conspecta, morabor
  deque meis manibus lora remissa fluent.

a quam paene Pelops Pisaea concidit hasta
  dum spectat vultus, Hippodamia, tuos!

nempe favore suae vicit tamen ille puellae—
  vincamus dominae quisque favore suae.

'Goddesses both' I hesitated, 'please listen.
I'm anxious not to offend either.

One of you does me the honour of high boots and a sceptre.
She has touched my tongue—I can feel my diction rising.

The other offers my love a name that will live. . . .
Well . . . the long and the short of it is—I choose her.

Grant your bard a breathing-space, Tragedy.
You need endless time and trouble. What *she* wants is short.'

The goddess relented. Hurry along there, Amorini.
Time presses. At my back I can sense a masterpiece.

ii

It's not the horses that bring me here
though I hope your favourite wins.

To sit with you and talk with you is why I've come—
I've come to tell you I'm in love.

If I watch you and you watch the races
we'll both enjoy watching a winner.

How I envy your charioteer!
He's a lucky man to be picked by you.

I wish it was me. I'd get my team
off to a flying start,

crack the whip, give them their heads
and shave the post with my nearside wheel.

But if I caught sight of *you* in the race
I'd drop the reins and lose ground.

Poor Pelops was nearly killed at Pisa
gazing in Hippodamia's eyes,

but being her favourite of course he won
as I hope your driver and I will.—

quid frustra refugis? cogit nos linea iungi.
    haec in lege loci commoda Circus habet.

tu tamen a dextra, quicumque es, parce puellae.
    contactu lateris laeditur illa tui.

tu quoque qui spectas post nos—tua contrahe crura
    si pudor est, rigido nec preme terga genu.

sed nimium demissa iacent tibi pallia terra.
    collige—vel digitis en ego tollo meis.

invida vestis eras quae tam bona crura tegebas!
    quoque magis spectes—invida vestis eras!

talia Milanion Atalantes crura fugacis
    optavit manibus sustinuisse suis.

talia pinguntur succinctae crura Dianae
    cum sequitur fortes fortior ipsa feras.

his ego non visis arsi—quid fiet ab ipsis?
    in flammam flammas, in mare fundis aquas.

suspicor ex istis et cetera posse placere
    quae bene sub tenui condita veste latent.

vis tamen interea faciles arcessere ventos
    quos faciet nostra mota tabella manu?

an magis hic meus est animi, non aeris, aestus,
    captaque femineus pectora torret amor?

dum loquor alba levi sparsa est tibi pulvere vestis—
    sordide de niveo corpore pulvis abi!

sed iam pompa venit. linguis animisque favete.
    tempus adest plausus. aurea pompa venit.

prima loco fertur passis Victoria pinnis—
    huc ades et meus hic fac, dea, vincat amor.

plaudite Neptuno, nimium qui creditis undis—
    nil mihi cum pelago, me mea terra capit.

plaude tuo Marti, miles—nos odimus arma;
    pax iuvat et media pace repertus amor.

It's no good edging away. The line brings us together—
that's the advantage of the seating here.

You on the right, sir—please be careful.
Your elbow's hurting the lady.

And you in the row behind—sit up, sir!
Your knees are digging into her back.

My dear, your dress is trailing on the ground.
Lift it up—or there you are, I've done it for you.

What mean material to hide those legs!
Yes, the more one looks the meaner it seems.

Legs like Atalanta,
Milanion's dream of bliss.

A painter's model for Diana
running wilder than the beasts.

My blood was on fire before. What happens now?
You're fuelling a furnace, flooding the Red Sea.

I'm sure that lightweight dress is hiding
still more delightful revelations.

But what about a breath of air while we wait?
This programme will do as a fan.

Is it really as hot as I feel? Or merely my imagination
fired by your sultry presence?

Just then a speck of dust fell on your white dress.
Forgive me—out, damned spot!

But here's the procession. Everybody hush.
Give them a hand. The golden procession's here.

First comes Victory, wings outstretched.
Goddess, grant me victory in love!

Neptune next. Salute him, sailors.
Not for me the ocean—I'm a landlover.

Soldiers, salute Mars. I'm a disarmer,
all for peace and amorous plenty.

125

auguribus Phoebus, Phoebe venantibus adsit.
　artifices in te verte, Minerva, manus.

ruricolae, Cereri teneroque adsurgite Baccho.
　Pollucem pugiles, Castora placet eques.

nos tibi, blanda Venus, puerisque potentibus arcu
　plaudimus. inceptis adnue, diva, meis

daque novae mentem dominae, patiatur amari—
　adnuit et motu signa secunda dedit.

quod dea promisit promittas ipsa rogamus—
　pace loquar Veneris, tu dea maior eris.

per tibi tot iuro testes pompamque deorum
　te dominam nobis tempus in omne peti.

sed pendent tibi crura. potes, si forte iuvabit,
　cancellis primos inseruisse pedes.

maxima iam vacuo praetor spectacula Circo
　quadriiugos aequo carcere misit equos.

cui studeas video. vincet cuicumque favebis.
　quid cupias ipsi scire videntur equi.

me miserum, metam spatioso circuit orbe.
　quid facis? admoto proxumus axe subit.

quid facis, infelix? perdis bona vota puellae.
　tende, precor, valida lora sinistra manu.

favimus ignavo. sed enim revocate, Quirites,
　et date iactatis undique signa togis.

en revocant. at ne turbet toga mota capillos,
　in nostros abdas te licet usque sinus.

iamque patent iterum reserato carcere postes.
　evolat admissis discolor agmen equis.

nunc saltem supera spatioque insurge patenti.
　sint mea, sint dominae fac rata vota meae.

sunt dominae rata vota meae—mea vota supersunt.
　ille tenet palmam—palma petenda mea est.

There's Phoebus for the soothsayers, Phoebe for the hunters,
Minerva for the master craftsmen.

Farmers can greet Bacchus and Ceres,
boxers pray to Pollux and knights to Castor.

But I salute the queen of love and the boy with the bow.
Venus, smile on my latest venture.

Make my new mistress willing—or weak-willed.
A lucky sign—the goddess nodded

giving her promise. And now I'm asking for yours.
With Venus' permission I'll worship *you*.

By all these witnesses, divine and human,
I swear I want you to be mine for ever.

But the seat's a bit too high for you.
Why not rest your feet on the railing in front?

Now, they've cleared the course. The Praetor's starting the first race.
Four-horse chariots. Look—they're off.

There's your driver. Anyone *you* back is bound to win.
Even the horses seem to know what you want.

My God, he's taking the corner too wide.
What are you doing? The man behind is drawing level.

What are you doing, wretch? Breaking a poor girl's heart.
For pity's sake pull on your left rein!

We've backed a loser. Come on everyone, all together,
flap your togas and signal a fresh start.

Look, they're calling them back. Lean your head against me
so the waving togas don't disarrange your hair.

Now, they're off again—plunging out of the stalls,
rushing down the course in a clash of colours.

Now's your chance to take the lead. Go all out for that gap.
Give my girl and me what we want.

Hurrah, he's done it! You've got what you wanted, sweetheart.
That only leaves me—do I win too?

risit, et argutis quiddam promisit ocellis.
  hoc satis hic. alio cetera redde loco.'

iii

Esse deos i crede! fidem iurata fefellit
  et facies illi quae fuit ante manet.

quam longos habuit nondum periura capillos
  tam longos postquam numina laesit habet.

candida, candorem roseo suffusa rubore,
  ante fuit—niveo lucet in ore rubor.

pes erat exiguus—pedis est artissima forma.
  longa decensque fuit—longa decensque manet.

argutos habuit—radiant ut sidus ocelli
  per quos mentita est perfida saepe mihi.

scilicet aeterni falsum iurare puellis
  di quoque concedunt, formaque numen habet.

perque suos illam nuper iurasse recordor
  perque meos oculos—et doluere mei.

dicite, di, si vos impune fefellerat illa,
  alterius meriti cur ego damna tuli?

non satis invidiae vobis Cepheia virgo est
  pro male formosa iussa parente mori?

non satis est quod vos habui sine pondere testes
  et mecum lusos ridet inulta deos?

ut sua per nostram redimat periuria poenam,
  victima deceptus decipientis ero?

aut sine re nomen deus est frustraque timetur
  et stulta populos credulitate movet,

aut, si quis deus est, teneras amat ille puellas—
  nimirum solas omnia posse iubet.

She's smiling. There's a promise in those bright eyes.
Let's leave now. You can pay my bet in private.

iii

Gods? There are none.
Or how could she break her solemn oath and keep her beauty?

Her waist-long hair is as long today
as before she flouted the Almighty.

In her face the lily and the rose
are glowing still—snow-white, pale red.

Her feet are still small and slender,
her figure lithe and lovely.

Her flashing eyes still shine like stars
though forsworn so often.—

Of course. Beauty is divine. Even the deathless gods
forgive a lovely woman's lies.

Lately she swore an oath, by the eyes of both of us,
but mine were the ones to suffer.

Great Gods, if you forgive her perjuries
why make me pay for them?

Is it not shame enough you ordered Andromeda
to die for the sin of her ugly mother?

Is it not shame enough you ignored my cry for help
and let her fool us both and laugh about it?

Can she also redeem her deceit at my expense? Must I
doubly deceived stand in for my deceiver?—

Either God is an empty word, a false terror
to overawe the credulous crowd,

or if he exists he's in love with the girls
and surrenders omnipotence to them.

129

nobis fatifero Mavors accingitur ense,
　　nos petit invicta Palladis hasta manu,

nobis flexibiles curvantur Apollinis arcus,
　　in nos alta Iovis dextera fulmen habet;

formosas superi metuunt offendere laesi
　　atque ultro quae se non timuere timent!

et quisquam pia tura focis imponere curat?
　　certe plus animi debet inesse viris.

Iuppiter igne suo lucos iaculatur et arces
　　missaque periuras tela ferire vetat.

tot meruere peti—Semele miserabilis arsit.
　　officio est illi poena reperta suo.

at si venturo se subduxisset amanti,
　　non pater in Baccho matris haberet opus.

quid queror et toti facio convicia caelo?
　　di quoque habent oculos, di quoque pectus habent.

si deus ipse forem, numen sine fraude liceret
　　femina mendaci falleret ore meum.

ipse ego iurarem verum iurasse puellas
　　et non de tetricis dicerer esse deus.

tu tamen illorum moderatius utere dono,
　　aut oculis certe parce, puella, meis.

iv

Dure vir, imposito tenerae custode puellae
　　nil agis—ingenio est quaeque tuenda suo.

si qua metu dempto casta est, ea denique casta est.
　　quae quia non liceat non facit, illa facit.

ut iam servaris bene corpus, adultera mens est,
　　nec custodiri ne velit ulla potest.

AMORES III iii 27–iv 6

Against us men Mars buckles on his blade
and Pallas hurls her spear.

Against us men Apollo bends his bow
and Jupiter aims his bolt.

But slighted Gods are afraid to offend the girls—
Beauty's assurance terrifies them.

Then why bother to burn incense?
We men should show more spirit.

Jupiter's lightning strikes his own high places
but he takes good care to miss the perjured sex.

When thousands deserved his bolt only poor Semele
went up in flames—killed for being kind.

Yet had she refused her lover
his maternal side would never have developed.—

But why complain? Why hurl abuse at the pantheon?
Gods too have eyes, Gods too have tender hearts.

If I were God I'd give the girls a licence
to lie and take my name in vain.

As a broad-minded Olympian
I'd even swear they'd sworn truly.

But sweetheart don't abuse your divine right
or in future at least go easy on my eyes.

iv

It's no good guarding a pretty girl, you big bully.
Her own instinct ought to protect her.

The chastity of fear is fake,
and forced refusal a form of consent.

However strictly you guard her body her thoughts can lust.
You can't imprison a woman's will.

131

nec corpus servare potes, licet omnia claudas—
    omnibus occlusis intus adulter erit.

cui peccare licet peccat minus. ipsa potestas
    semina nequitiae languidiora facit.

desine, crede mihi, vitia inritare vetando;
    obsequio vinces aptius illa tuo.

vidi ego nuper equum contra sua vincla tenacem
    ore reluctanti fulminis ire modo;

constitit ut primum concessas sensit habenas
    frenaque in effusa laxa iacere iuba.

nitimur in vetitum semper cupimusque negata;
    sic interdictis imminet aeger aquis.

centum fronte oculos, centum cervice gerebat
    Argus, et hos unus saepe fefellit Amor.

in thalamum Danae ferro saxoque perennem
    quae fuerat virgo tradita, mater erat.

Penelope mansit, quamvis custode carebat,
    inter tot iuvenis intemerata procos.

quidquid servatur cupimus magis, ipsaque furem
    cura vocat. pauci quod sinit alter amant.

nec facie placet illa sua sed amore mariti.
    nescioquid quod te ceperit esse putant.

non proba fit quam vir servat sed adultera cara.
    ipse timor pretium corpore maius habet.

indignere licet, iuvat inconcessa voluptas;
    sola placet 'timeo' dicere si qua potest.

nec tamen ingenuam ius est servare puellam;
    hic metus externae corpora gentis agat.

scilicet ut possit custos 'ego' dicere 'feci',
    in laudem servi casta sit illa tui?

rusticus est nimium quem laedit adultera coniunx,
    et notos mores non satis Vrbis habet,

With all your locks you can't even guard her body—
she'll find a lover among the household.

If you let her sin she'll be less of a sinner.
Responsibility takes the kick out of free love.

If I were you I shouldn't encourage vice by veto;
you'll find concession a stronger deterrent.

The other day I watched a horse on a tight rein—
he took the bit between his teeth and bolted,

but stopped dead the moment he felt the reins relax
and drop loose on his flying mane.

We're all rebels against restriction—in love with the illicit—
sick men craving the fluid they're forbidden.

Argus had eyes in the back of his head—hundreds of them,
but Cupid tricked him single-handed.

Into her bower of stone and steel Danae entered
virginal—to emerge a mother.

But Penelope kept faith without a guard
among that crowd of young suitors.

Locked up means more desirable. Security
is a challenge to thieves. Few can love by another man's leave.

Your wife's beauty is less of a draw than your passion for her—
she's got something special, we think, to hold you.

By being possessive you make her more worthwhile as a mistress;
in fact her fear counts for more than her figure.

Storm as you please, forbidden fruit is sweet.
The woman who says 'I daren't' is the one for me.

However you've no right to imprison a free-born girl.
Such sanctions are for foreigners only.

And her warder will say it's thanks to him. Do you want a slave
to take the credit for her chastity?

To fret about adultery is too provincial
and shows ignorance of Roman manners—

133

in qua Martigenae non sunt sine crimine nati,
    Romulus Iliades Iliadesque Remus.

quo tibi formosam si non nisi casta placebat?
    non possunt ullis ista coire modis.

si sapis, indulge dominae vultusque severos
    exue nec rigidi iura tuere viri,

et cole quos dederit—multos dabit—uxor amicos.
    gratia sic minimo magna labore venit,

sic poteris iuvenum convivia semper inire,
    et quae non dederis multa videre domi.

V

'Nox erat et somnus lassos submisit ocellos.
    terruerunt animum talia visa meum.

colle sub aprico creberrimus ilice lucus
    stabat et in ramis multa latebat avis.

area gramineo suberat viridissima prato,
    umida de guttis lene sonantis aquae.

ipse sub arboreis vitabam frondibus aestum,
    fronde sub arborea sed tamen aestus erat.

ecce petens variis immixtas floribus herbas
    constitit ante oculos candida vacca meos,

candidior nivibus tum cum cecidere recentes,
    in liquidas nondum quas mora vertit aquas,

candidior, quod adhuc spumis stridentibus albet
    et modo siccatam, lacte, reliquit ovem.

taurus erat comes huic, feliciter ille maritus,
    cumque sua teneram coniuge pressit humum.

dum iacet et lente revocatas ruminat herbas
    atque iterum pasto pascitur ante cibo,

after all, the Martian twins were born out of wedlock,
Ilia's children, Romulus and Remus.

Why marry good looks if all you wanted was good behaviour?
The two things never mix.

Be sensible and give in to her. Stop being a prig.
Don't press your rights as a husband,

but cultivate the many friends she'll bring you.
You'll reap a rich reward for doing nothing,

go out when you like to all the gay parties,
or stay at home and enjoy the presents you never gave her.

V

'I was tired that night and sleep came soon
bringing a dreadful dream.

I dreamt of a grove of ilex, under a sunny hill,
alive with birds among the leaves,

and a green meadow where the trees ended,
and a murmuring of water.

I was sheltering from the heat, there in the shade of the leaves
—though the leafy shade gave little shelter—

when a white heifer looking for sweet grasses and flowers
halted in front of me.

Whiter than snow she was
when it lies new-fallen,

whiter than sheep's milk at milking time
when it froths in the pail.

A bull, her happy mate, followed
and lay down at her side,

lay there peacefully feeding,
slowly chewing the cud

visus erat somno vires adimente ferendi
   cornigerum terra deposuisse caput.

hic levibus cornix pinnis delapsa per auras
   venit et in viridi garrula sedit humo

terque bovis niveae petulanti pectora rostro
   fodit et albentes abstulit ore iubas.

illa locum taurumque diu cunctata reliquit
   (sed niger in vaccae pectore livor erat)

utque procul vidit carpentes pabula tauros
   (carpebant tauri pabula laeta procul)

illuc se rapuit gregibusque immiscuit illis
   et petiit herbae fertilioris humum.

dic age, nocturnae quicumque es imaginis augur,
   si quid habent veri visa, quid ista ferant.'

sic ego. nocturnae sic dixit imaginis augur
   expendens animo singula dicta suo:

'quem tu mobilibus foliis vitare volebas
   sed male vitabas, aestus amoris erat.

vacca puella tua est—aptus color ille puellae.
   tu vir et in vacca compare taurus eras.

pectora quod rostro cornix fodiebat acuto,
   ingenium dominae lena movebit anus.

quod cunctata diu taurum sua vacca reliquit,
   frigidus in viduo destituere toro.

livor et adverso maculae sub pectore nigrae
   pectus adulterii labe carere negant.'

dixerat interpres. gelido mihi sanguis ab ore
   fugit et ante oculos nox stetit alta meos.

till sleep relaxed his powerful neck
and his heavy head sank to the ground.

Then a carrion crow glided down
landing with a loud caw,

pecked the heifer's breast three times and flew away
with a tuft of snow-white hair in her beak.

The heifer at long last abandoned mate and meadow
(her breast now marked with a black bruise)

and seeing bulls in the distance grazing
(there were several grazing in the green distance)

hurried over to join them
in hope of richer grass.

Now tell me, my unknown interpreter of dreams,
if dreams have meaning what does this one mean?'

The interpreter weighed my words
and gave me this reply:

'The heat you tried in vain to avoid
under the restless leaves was love.

The heifer your girl—snow-white for purity.
The bull her lover—you.

The carrion crow pecking her breast
a Madam trying to corrupt her.

As the heifer at long last left her mate
so you will be left—in a cold bed.

The bruise on her breast, those black marks,
are the stain of adultery deep in her heart.'

At this interpretation my blood ran cold
and a great darkness covered my eyes.

vi

Amnis harundinibus limosas obsite ripas,
    ad dominam propero—siste parumper aquas.

nec tibi sunt pontes nec quae sine remigis ictu
    concava traiecto cumba rudente vehat.

parvus eras, memini, nec te transire refugi,
    summaque vix talos contigit unda meos.

nunc ruis adposito nivibus de monte solutis
    et turpi crassas gurgite volvis aquas.

quid properasse iuvat, quid parca dedisse quieti
    tempora, quid nocti conseruisse diem,

si tamen hic standum est, si non datur artibus ullis
    ulterior nostro ripa premenda pede?

nunc ego quas habuit pinnas Danaeius heros
    terribili densum cum tulit angue caput,

nunc opto currum de quo Cerealia primum
    semina venerunt in rude missa solum.

prodigiosa loquor, veterum mendacia vatum,
    nec tulit haec umquam nec feret ulla dies.

tu potius, ripis effuse capacibus amnis—
    sic aeternus eas—labere fine tuo.

non eris invidiae, torrens, mihi crede, ferendae
    si dicar per te forte retentus amans.

flumina debebant iuvenes in amore iuvare.
    flumina senserunt ipsa quid esset amor.

Inachus in Melie Bithynide pallidus isse
    dicitur et gelidis incaluisse vadis.

nondum Troia fuit lustris obsessa duobus
    cum rapuit vultus, Xanthe, Neaera tuos.

Halt, muddy river! Rest awhile among your reeds.
Make way for a lover in a hurry,

for you haven't a bridge, or a chain-ferry,
to take me across without oars.

I remember you as a little stream, easily forded,
hardly deep enough to wet my ankles.

Now you're in spate, swollen by melting snow from the mountain,
swirling along brown and turbid.

Why did I hurry, scanting sleep,
journeying night and day,

to mark time here, without a hope
of setting foot on the far bank?

O for the wings of the hero
who cut off Medusa's head!

O for the flying wagon
that scattered the first seed!

Signs and wonders, poetic lies—
lost in the daylight of the present.

Listen, swollen river: if you want to roll on for ever
roll on within limits.

Your name will be mud if the tale gets round
that you crossed a poet in love.

Rivers should help young lovers—
rivers too have loved.

Inachus turned pale for Melia—
she warmed his chilly bed.

Before the famous fall of Troy
Xanthus fell for Neaera.

139

quid? non Alpheon diversis currere terris
    virginis Arcadiae certus adegit amor?

te quoque promissam Xutho, Penee, Creusam
    Pthiotum terris occuluisse ferunt.

quid referam Asopon, quem cepit Martia Thebe,
    natarum Thebe quinque futura parens?

cornua si tua nunc ubi sint, Acheloe, requiram,
    Herculis irata fracta querere manu—

nec tanti Calydon, nec tota Aetolia tanti,
    una tamen tanti Deianira fuit.

ille fluens dives septena per ostia Nilus,
    qui patriam tantae tam bene celat aquae,

fertur in Evanthe collectam Asopide flammam
    vincere gurgitibus non potuisse suis.

siccus ut amplecti Salmonida posset Enipeus
    cedere iussit aquam—iussa recessit aqua.

nec te praetereo qui per cava saxa volutans
    Tiburis Argei pomifer arva rigas,

Ilia cui placuit, quamvis erat horrida cultu,
    ungue notata comas, ungue notata genas.

illa gemens patruique nefas delictaque Martis
    errabat nudo per loca sola pede.

hanc Anien rapidis animosus vidit ab undis
    raucaque de mediis sustulit ora vadis,

atque ita 'quid nostras' dixit 'teris anxia ripas,
    Ilia ab Idaeo Laomedonte genus?

quo cultus abiere tui? quid sola vagaris,
    vitta nec evinctas impedit alba comas?

quid fles et madidos lacrimis corrumpis ocellos
    pectoraque insana plangis aperta manu?

ille habet et silices et vivum in pectore ferrum
    qui tenero lacrimas lentus in ore videt.

AMORES III vi 29–60

Alpheus ran to Syracuse
after his true love Arethusa.

Peneus kidnapped a bride
and smuggled her into Phthia.

Asopus adored Thebe—
Thebe the mother of five girls.

Where are the horns of Achelous?
Broken, by angry Heracles,

not for Calydon, not for all Aetolia,
but for Deianira the one and only.

Rich father Nile, river of seven mouths
guarding the secret of his rising,

couldn't smother with his flood
the flame Evanthe kindled.

Enipeus gave the order *Waters, about turn!*
and, when they turned about, drily embraced Salmonis.

And don't forget the river tumbling down the rocks
by Tivoli's orchards

the river that fell for Ilia, though she was distraught,
tearing her hair in grief, tearing her cheeks in cruel grief,

mourning the sin of Mars and the crime of Amulius,
wandering barefoot in the wilderness.

Impetuous Anio, seeing her, raised his head
from the rushing waters in rough greeting:

'Ilia, daughter of Ilion's kings,
why do you walk forlorn along my banks?

Why do you wander alone, in mourning,
with no white headband to bind your hair?

Why do you weep and dim those melting eyes with tears
and lacerate your lovely breasts?

Flint-hearted, steely-fleshed is he
who sees your tears and feels no pity.

Ilia, pone metus. tibi regia nostra patebit
  teque colent amnes. Ilia, pone metus.

tu centum aut plures inter dominabere nymphas,
  nam centum aut plures flumina nostra tenent.

ne me sperne, precor, tantum, Troiana propago.
  munera promissis uberiora feres.'

dixerat. illa oculos in humum deiecta modestos
  spargebat tepido flebilis imbre sinus.

ter molita fugam ter ad altas restitit undas,
  currendi vires eripiente metu.

sera tamen scindens inimico pollice crinem
  edidit indignos ore tremente sonos:

'o utinam mea lecta forent patrioque sepulcro
  condita cum poterant virginis ossa legi!

cur, modo Vestalis, taedas invitor ad ullas
  turpis et Iliacis infitianda focis?

quid moror et digitis designor adultera vulgi?
  desint famosus quae notet ora pudor.'

hactenus, et vestem tumidis praetendit ocellis
  atque ita se in rapidas perdita misit aquas.

supposuisse manus ad pectora lubricus amnis
  dicitur et socii iura dedisse tori.—

te quoque credibile est aliqua caluisse puella,
  sed nemora et silvae crimina vestra tegunt.

dum loquor increvit latis spatiosior undis
  nec capit admissas alveus altus aquas.

quid mecum, furiose, tibi? quid mutua differs
  gaudia? quid coeptum, rustice, rumpis iter?

quid si legitimum flueres, si nobile flumen,
  si tibi per terras maxima fama foret?

nomen habes nullum, rivis collecte caducis,
  nec tibi sunt fontes nec tibi certa domus.

AMORES III vi 61–92

Ilia, don't be afraid. My palace is waiting for you.
My waters will pay you homage. Ilia, don't be afraid.

You shall be queen of a hundred nymphs—or more,
for a hundred or more live in my stream.

Oh Trojan princess, don't disdain me
but find fulfilment—richer than I've promised.'

She dared not look up to answer;
the warm tears were raining down.

She tried to escape, but couldn't move from the river bank.
Fear had robbed her of strength to run.

Trembling, tearing her hair,
she spoke at last—these bitter words:

'Would I had died a virgin
and lay in my father's tomb!

Why am I offered the torch of marriage—
a Vestal who broke her vows, an outcast of Vesta's flame?

Why live on to be pointed at by vulgar fingers?
Death to the face that shame has branded.'

So saying she held her stole in front of her eyes
and threw herself in the rushing torrent.

But the king of the river slid his hands under her breasts
and made her his queen consort.—

You too, I suppose, have warmed to a woman's flesh,
but these woods conceal your wicked ways.

While I've been talking your waters have spread wider—
your channel isn't deep enough to hold them.

What makes you so wild against me—delaying my delight,
rudely breaking my journey?

It might be different if you were on the map,
a genuine river, known to the world:

but you're a nameless inundation,
a vagrant of no fixed source,

fontis habes instar pluviamque nivesque solutas,
    quas tibi divitias pigra ministrat hiemps.

aut lutulentus agis brumali tempore cursus
    aut premis arentem pulverulentus humum.

quis te tum potuit sitiens haurire viator?
    quis dixit grata voce 'perennis eas'?

damnosus pecori curris, damnosior agris;
    forsitan haec alios, me mea damna movent.

huic ego vae demens narrabam fluminum amores!
    iactasse indigne nomina tanta pudet.

nescioquem hunc spectans Acheloon et Inachon amnem
    et potui nomen, Nile, referre tuum!

at tibi pro meritis opto, non candide torrens,
    sint rapidi soles siccaque semper hiemps.

vii

At non formosa est, at non bene culta puella,
    at puto non votis saepe petita meis!

hanc tamen in nullos tenui male languidus usus
    sed iacui pigro crimen onusque toro

nec potui cupiens, pariter cupiente puella,
    inguinis effeti parte iuvante frui.

illa quidem nostro subiecit eburnea collo
    bracchia, Sithonia candidiora nive,

osculaque inseruit cupide luctantia linguis
    lascivum femori supposuitque femur

et mihi blanditias dixit dominumque vocavit
    et quae praeterea publica verba iuvant.

tacta tamen veluti gelida mea membra cicuta
    segnia propositum destituere meum.

rising in rains and melting snows,
the idle wealth of winter.

In December a muddy torrent,
a dust bath in July

without a drop to wet a traveller's whistle
or earn a beggar's blessing.

In spate a loss to cattle, and a greater loss to crops—
though it's my loss that matters now.

I must have been crazy telling you tales of rivers in love.
I'm ashamed to have dropped the names

of Inachus and Nile and Achelous
in front of such a nondescript.

Mean and muddy torrent, I wish you all you deserve:
drought in winter, and in summer—heat waves.

vii

No, I must face facts:
she was lovely—she was glamorous—I was mad about her.

But there I lay, with this girl in my arms, and nothing happened.
The position was absurd.

I wanted it badly enough, and so did she—
but could I rise to the occasion?

Ivory-smooth her arms embraced me—
whiter than snow in sunshine.

Thigh to thigh she kissed me—
deep kisses, alive with desire—

whispered temptation, called me lord and master,
ran through the erotic rosary.

But my body was paralyzed
as though I had drunk hemlock—

truncus iners iacui, species et inutile pondus,
　　et non exactum corpus an umbra forem.

quae mihi ventura est, siquidem ventura, senectus
　　cum desit numeris ipsa iuventa suis?

a pudet annorum. quo me iuvenemque virumque?
　　nec iuvenem nec me sensit amica virum.

sic flammas aditura pias aeterna sacerdos
　　surgit et a caro fratre verenda soror.

at nuper bis flava Chlide, ter candida Pitho,
　　ter Libas officio continuata meo est.

exigere a nobis angusta nocte Corinnam,
　　me memini numeros sustinuisse novem.

num mea Thessalico languent devota veneno
　　corpora? num misero carmen et herba nocent?

sagave poenicea defixit nomina cera
　　et medium tenuis in iecur egit acus?

carmine laesa Ceres sterilem vanescit in herbam,
　　deficiunt laesi carmine fontis aquae,

ilicibus glandes cantataque vitibus uva
　　decidit et nullo poma movente fluunt:

quid vetat et nervos magicas torpere per artes?
　　forsitan impatiens sit latus inde meum.

huc pudor accessit. facti pudor ipse nocebat.
　　ille fuit vitii causa secunda mei.

at qualem vidi tantum tetigique puellam!
　　sic etiam tunica tangitur illa sua.

illius ad tactum Pylius iuvenescere possit
　　Tithonusque annis fortior esse suis.

haec mihi contigerat sed vir non contigit illi.
　　quas nunc concipiam per nova vota preces?

credo etiam magnos quo sum tam turpiter usus
　　muneris oblati paenituisse deos.

lying there like a lay figure.
Was it really me—or my ghost?

So much for fine upstanding youth. And when I grow old—
if I grow old—what then?

Youth and virility—what humiliation!
For all she could tell I had neither.

She left the bed like one of Vesta's nuns
or a sister from her little brother's side.

But the other day I took Chlide twice,
Pitho three times, Libas three,

and as for Corinna—she inspired my record:
in one short night I counted nine.

Could some witch have laid me under a spell?
Given me a magical decoction?

Moulded my image in red wax
and stuck pins in its guts?

Magic can turn a wheat-field into weed,
drain well-springs dry,

make grapes and chestnuts drop,
strip fruit trees bare.

Couldn't it also emasculate muscle?
Yes, it was probably witchcraft—

that, and humiliation too—
aggravating the collapse.

God, what a lovely girl! But I just gazed and clung—
close as a brassière to her breasts.

Her touch could have made a Nestor young again,
resurrected a Tithonus.

Perfection was in my grasp—and a sham in hers.
What have I left to pray for?

The gods must surely regret the gift
I used so badly.

optabam certe recipi—sum nempe receptus.
  oscula ferre—tuli. proximus esse—fui.

quo mihi fortunae tantum? quo regna sine usu?
  quid nisi possedi dives avarus opes?

sic aret mediis taciti vulgator in undis
  pomaque quae nullo tempore tangat habet.

a tenera quisquam sic surgit mane puella
  protinus ut sanctos possit adire deos?

sed puto non †blanda†, non optima perdidit in me
  oscula, non omni sollicitavit ope?

illa graves potuit quercus adamantaque durum
  surdaque blanditiis saxa movere suis.

digna movere fuit certe vivosque virosque—
  sed neque tum vixi nec vir ut ante fui.

quid iuvet ad surdas si cantet Phemius aures?
  quid miserum Thamyran picta tabella iuvet?

at quae non tacita formavi gaudia mente!
  quos ego non finxi disposuique modos!

nostra tamen iacuere velut praemortua membra
  turpiter, hesterna languidiora rosa.

quae nunc, ecce, vigent intempestiva valentque;
  nunc opus exposcunt militiamque suam.

quin istic pudibunda iaces, pars pessima nostri?
  sic sum pollicitis captus et ante tuis.

tu dominum fallis. per te deprensus inermis
  tristia cum magno damna pudore tuli.

hanc etiam non est mea dedignata puella
  molliter admota sollicitare manu.

sed postquam nullas consurgere posse per artes
  immemoremque sui procubuisse videt,

'quid me ludis?' ait 'quis te, male sane, iubebat
  invitum nostro ponere membra toro?

I wanted a welcome—and got it. To kiss her—and I did.
Be alone with her—and I was.

I had all the luck and nothing came of it—
ownership without possession—a miser's million—

Tantalus parched in his pool,
clutching the unattainable.

I left her pure as the day I was born,
pure enough to enter a temple.

She kissed me high, and she kissed me low—
she tried everything.

She could have moved an oak, softened a stone,
melted adamant,

let alone roused all living men—
but I was neither man nor alive,

and she was Sappho singing to the deaf,
an artist's model posing for the blind.

Though I filled my mind with erotic pictures
and imagined a hundred variations,

I lay there limp and lifeless—
yesterday's drooping rose.

Now of course it's quite different—long and strong,
spoiling for battle, eager to join up.

Lie down, dog!
I've been had like this before.

You tricked me, left me in the lurch,
put me to shame—not to mention expense.

And think of the trouble she took with you—
her delicate handling of my problem.

But you wouldn't budge—not one half-inch.
You took not the slightest notice of her.

'Stop fooling about' she said. 'What's the matter with you?
Who sent you along to lie down here?

aut te traiectis Aeaea venefica Ianis
   devovet aut alio lassus amore venis.'

nec mora, desiluit tunica velata soluta
   (et decuit nudos proripuisse pedes)

neve suae possent intactam scire ministrae
   dedecus hoc sumpta dissimulavit aqua.

viii

Et quisquam ingenuas etiam nunc suspicit artes
   aut tenerum dotes carmen habere putat?

ingenium quondam fuerat pretiosius auro,
   at nunc barbaria est grandis habere nihil.

cum pulchre dominae nostri placuere libelli,
   quo licuit libris non licet ire mihi.

cum bene laudavit, laudato ianua clausa est.
   turpiter huc illuc ingeniosus eo.

ecce recens dives parto per vulnera censu
   praefertur nobis—sanguine pastus eques.

hunc potes amplecti formosis, vita, lacertis?
   huius in amplexu, vita, iacere potes?

si nescis, caput hoc galeam portare solebat,
   ense latus cinctum quod tibi servit erat.

laeva manus, cui nunc serum male convenit aurum,
   scuta tulit. dextram tange—cruenta fuit.

qua periit aliquis potes hanc contingere dextram?
   heu ubi mollities pectoris illa tui?

cerne cicatrices, veteris vestigia pugnae—
   quaesitum est illi corpore quicquid habet.

forsitan et quotiens hominem iugulaverit ille
   indicet—hoc fassas tangis, avara, manus?

Either you've been bewitched
or you've just left another woman.'

With that she leapt out of bed,
barefoot, in a flurry of dressing-gown,

and to prevent the maids from guessing
camouflaged disgrace with a little water.

viii

Does anyone these days respect the artist
or value elegiac verse?

Time was when imagination meant more than money
but today *poor* and *boor* mean the same thing.

'I adore your poetry' she says,
and allows it in where I can't follow.

After the compliments the door curtly closes
and I, her poet, moon about humiliated,

displaced by a new-rich upstart, a bloody soldier
who butchered his way to wealth and a knighthood.

Him in your lovely arms! You in his clutches!
Light of my life, how could you?

That head wore a helmet, remember—
that obliging flank a sword.

His left hand, flashing the new equestrian ring,
once gripped a shield. His right has killed.

How can you hold hands with a killer?
Have you no sensibility?

Look at his scars, marks of a brutal trade—
that body earned him all he has.

I expect he even brags about his killings.
How can you touch him after that, gold-digger,

ille ego Musarum purus Phoebique sacerdos
   ad rigidas canto carmen inane fores?

discite, qui sapitis, non quae nos scimus inertes
   sed trepidas acies et fera castra sequi,

proque bono versu primum deducite pilum.
   nox tibi, si belles, possit, Homere, dari.

Iuppiter admonitus nihil esse potentius auro
   corruptae pretium virginis ipse fuit.

dum merces aberat, durus pater, ipsa severa,
   aerati postes, ferrea turris erat,

sed postquam sapiens in munere venit adulter,
   praebuit ipsa sinus et dare iussa dedit.

at cum regna senex caeli Saturnus haberet,
   omne lucrum tenebris alta premebat humus,

aeraque et argentum cumque auro pondera ferri
   Manibus admorat, nullaque massa fuit.

at meliora dabat—curvo sine vomere fruges
   pomaque et in quercu mella reperta cava.

nec valido quisquam terras scindebat aratro,
   signabat nullo limite mensor humum,

non freta demisso verrebant eruta remo,
   ultima mortali tum via litus erat.

contra te sollers, hominum natura, fuisti
   et nimium damnis ingeniosa tuis.

quo tibi turritis incingere moenibus urbes?
   quo tibi discordes addere in arma manus?

quid tibi cum pelago? terra contenta fuisses.
   cur non et caelum tertia regna facis?

qua licet adfectas caelum quoque—templa Quirinus,
   Liber et Alcides et modo Caesar habent.

eruimus terra solidum pro frugibus aurum.
   possidet inventas sanguine miles opes.

AMORES III viii 23–54

and allow me, the priest of Phoebus and the Muses,
to serenade your locked door in vain?

No man of taste should waste his time on art—
he'd better enlist and rough it under canvas.

Don't turn out couplets, turn out on parade.
Homer, join up if you want a date!

Jove Almighty realized gold's omnipotence
when he cashed himself to seduce a girl.

Before the transaction father looked grim, daughter prudish,
her turret steely, the doorposts coppered.

But when the crafty lecher arrived in cash
she opened her lap and gave as golden as she got.

Long ago, when Saturn ruled in the kingdom of heaven,
Earth sank all her capital in darkness—

stowed bronze and silver, gold and heavy iron in hell.
Ingots were not yet known:

she had better things to offer—crops without cultivation,
fruit on the bough, honey in the hollow oak.

No one tore the ground with ploughshares
or parcelled out the land

or swept the sea with dipping oars—
the shore was the world's end.

Clever human nature, victim of your inventions,
disastrously creative,

why cordon cities with towered walls?
Why arm for war?

Why take to the sea—as if happiness were far away?
Why not annex the sky too?

We have, in a modest way—by deifying Bacchus
and Hercules and Romulus and now Caesar.

We dig for gold instead of food.
Our soldiers earn blood-money.

curia pauperibus clausa est. dat census honores—
    inde gravis iudex, inde severus eques.

omnia possideant—illis Campusque Forumque
    serviat, hi pacem crudaque bella gerant—

tantum ne nostros avidi liceantur amores
    et—satis est—aliquid pauperis esse sinant.

at nunc, exaequet tetricas licet illa Sabinas,
    imperat ut captae qui dare multa potest.

me prohibet custos, in me timet illa maritum.
    si dederim, tota cedet uterque domo.

o si neclecti quisquam deus ultor amantis
    tam male quaesitas pulvere mutet opes!

ix

Memnona si mater, mater ploravit Achillem,
    et tangunt magnas tristia fata deas,

flebilis indignos, Elegia, solve capillos—
    a nimis ex vero nunc tibi nomen erit.

ille tui vates operis, tua fama, Tibullus
    ardet in exstructo corpus inane rogo.

ecce, puer Veneris fert eversamque pharetram
    et fractos arcus et sine luce facem.

aspice demissis ut eat miserabilis alis
    pectoraque infesta tundat aperta manu.

excipiunt lacrimas sparsi per colla capilli,
    oraque singultu concutiente sonant.

AMORES III viii 55–ix 12

The Senate's barred to the poor. Capital is king,
creates the solemn judge and the censorious knight.

Let them own the world—knights controlling Campus and Forum,
Senate dictating peace and war,

but hands off love! Sweethearts shouldn't be up for auction.
Leave the poor man his little corner.

As it is, if my girl were chaste as a Sabine prude
she'd crawl for anyone with money.

So I am locked out. When I'm around she's scared of her husband.
He'd vanish quick enough if I could pay.

O for a god in heaven to right a lover's wrongs
and turn those fat pickings to a pile of dust!

ix

If Thetis and Aurora
Shed tears for their dead sons,
If goddesses feel grief,
Loosen your hair and weep,
Gentle Elegia,
Sorrow's true namesake.
For the spent body of Tibullus
Your poet laureate
Is burning on the tall pyre,
And Cupid's bow is broken,
His quiver reversed,
His torch burnt out.
See how sadly he walks
With wings drooping,
Beating his breast.
And the tears fall
On his wild hair
And he sobs aloud,

155

fratris in Aeneae sic illum funere dicunt
    egressum tectis, pulcher Iule, tuis.

nec minus est confusa Venus moriente Tibullo
    quam iuveni rupit cum ferus inguen aper.

at sacri vates et divum cura vocamur;
    sunt etiam qui nos numen habere putent.

scilicet omne sacrum mors importuna profanat;
    omnibus obscuras inicit illa manus.

quid pater Ismario, quid mater profuit Orpheo?
    carmine quid victas obstipuisse feras?

et *Linon* in silvis idem pater *ailinon* altis
    dicitur invita concinuisse lyra.

adice Maeoniden, a quo ceu fonte perenni
    vatum Pieriis ora rigantur aquis—

hunc quoque summa dies nigro submersit Averno;
    defugiunt avidos carmina sola rogos,

durat opus tantum, Troiani fama laboris
    tardaque nocturno tela retexta dolo.

sic Nemesis longum, sic Delia nomen habebunt,
    altera cura recens, altera primus amor.

quid vos sacra iuvant? quid nunc Aegyptia prosunt
    sistra? quid in vacuo secubuisse toro?

cum rapiunt mala fata bonos—ignoscite fasso—
    sollicitor nullos esse putare deos.

As when he left Iulus' palace
Long ago
To follow his brother to the grave.
Venus too grieves for Tibullus
As she grieved for Adonis
When the wild boar ripped his groin.
'Dedicated poet',
'In God's keeping',
'Divinely inspired'—so run the phrases,
But Death mocks dedication
With the laying on
Of invisible hands.
What help were Phoebus and the Muse
To their son Orpheus?
What help the song that tamed wild beasts?
And did not Phoebus in the forest
Sing *Linos ailinos*
To the broken strings of his lyre?
Even Maeonian Homer,
Spring of the water of life
On the lips of poets,
Drowned at last
In black Avernus.
Only his verse evades the pyre,
A rumour of heroic war,
A deceiving web unravelled at night.
His megalith.
So Nemesis and Delia,
Last longing and first love,
Shall be live names,
Though Isis failed them
In a clacking of rattles,
An emptiness of lonely nights.
When evil overtakes the good,
To disbelieve in God
Can be forgiven.

vive pius—moriere. pius cole sacra—colentem
  Mors gravis a templis in cava busta trahet.

carminibus confide bonis—iacet, ecce, Tibullus;
  vix manet e tanto parva quod urna capit.

tene, sacer vates, flammae rapuere rogales?
  pectoribus pasci nec timuere tuis?

aurea sanctorum potuissent templa deorum
  urere, quae tantum sustinuere nefas.

avertit vultus Erycis quae possidet arces;
  sunt quoque qui lacrimas continuisse negant.

sed tamen hoc melius quam si Phaeacia tellus
  ignotum vili supposuisset humo.

hic certe madidos fugientis pressit ocellos
  mater et in cineres ultima dona tulit.

hic soror in partem misera cum matre doloris
  venit, inornatas dilaniata comas,

cumque tuis sua iunxerunt Nemesisque priorque
  oscula nec solos destituere rogos.

Delia discedens 'felicius' inquit 'amata
  sum tibi: vixisti dum tuus ignis eram.'

cui Nemesis 'quid' ait 'tibi sunt mea damna dolori?
  me tenuit moriens deficiente manu.'

si tamen e nobis aliquid nisi nomen et umbra
  restat, in Elysia valle Tibullus erit.

The decent life is death,
The decent worship—death,
Dragging you from high altar to hollow tomb.
Some trust in verse—
Let them look at Tibullus,
A little ash in a little urn.
Flames inspired
And flames destroyed him,
Eating his heart
In desecration
Worse than the gutting
Of a gilded shrine.
And Venus on the heights of Eryx
Looked away—
Hiding the tears perhaps.
But better to die in Rome
Than a stranger on Corfu
Thrust in a cheap grave.
Here at least his mother
Could close the blank eyes
And offer farewell gifts.
His sister could take part
In the ritual of grief,
Tearing dishevelled hair.
Nemesis and his first love
Could attend the pyre
And add their kisses.
'I was the lucky one'
Delia whispered at parting—
'My love gave you life.'
But Nemesis replied
'Not yours the loss.
He died with his hand in mine.'
And yet, if human survival
Is more than a haunting name,
Tibullus lives in Elysium,

obvius huic venies hedera iuvenalia cinctus
tempora cum Calvo, docte Catulle, tuo;

tu quoque, si falsum est temerati crimen amici,
sanguinis atque animae prodige Galle tuae.

his comes umbra tua est, siqua est modo corporis umbra;
auxisti numeros, culte Tibulle, pios.

ossa quieta, precor, tuta requiescite in urna,
et sit humus cineri non onerosa tuo.

X

Annua venerunt Cerealis tempora sacri;
secubat in vacua sola puella toro.
flava Ceres, tenues spicis redimita capillos,
cur inhibes sacris commoda nostra tuis?
te, dea, munificam gentes ubi quaeque loquuntur,
nec minus humanis invidet ulla bonis.
ante nec hirsuti torrebant farra coloni,
nec notum terris area nomen erat,
sed glandem quercus, oracula prima, ferebant—
haec erat et teneri caespitis herba cibus.
prima Ceres docuit turgescere semen in agris,
falce coloratas subsecuitque comas.
prima iugis tauros supponere colla coegit
et veterem curvo dente revellit humum.
hanc quisquam lacrimis laetari credit amantum
et bene tormentis secubituque coli?
nec tamen est, quamvis agros amet illa feraces,
rustica nec viduum pectus amoris habet.

Welcomed there by Calvus
And Catullus the scholar-poet,
Young men, ivy-garlanded—
By Gallus too, if the charge
Of friendship betrayed is false,
Gallus who flung away life and love.
To these rare spirits,
If the spirit lives,
Tibullus brings grace.
May his bones rest in peace,
Undisturbed in the urn,
And earth be no burden to his ashes.

X

These are the festival days of Ceres—
the nights my love must sleep alone.

Golden goddess, wearing the wheat in your silken hair,
why does your cult say No to pleasure?

Your name is Bountiful among all nations—
no goddess gives more generously.

Long ago, before unshaven peasants parched the corn,
before the threshing-floor was known,

when we lived off the oracular oak
and our food was acorns and a few herbs,

Ceres taught the first seed to sprout in the furrow
and the sickle to cut her yellow hair

and the ox to bend his neck to the yoke
and the plough's tooth to groove the ground.

Can she delight in lovers' tears?
In sackcloth and celibacy?

She's a country goddess but not uncouth—
she too has loved.

161

Cretes erunt testes. nec fingunt omnia Cretes.
  Crete nutrito terra superba Iove.

illic sideream mundi qui temperat arcem
  exiguus tenero lac bibit ore puer.

magna fides testi. testis laudatur alumno.
  fassuram Cererem crimina nota puto.

viderat Iasium Cretaea diva sub Ida
  figentem certa terga ferina manu.

vidit, et ut tenerae flammam rapuere medullae,
  hinc pudor, ex illa parte trahebat amor.

victus amore pudor. sulcos arere videres
  et sata cum minima parte redire sui.

cum bene iactati pulsarant arva ligones
  ruperat et duram vomer aduncus humum

seminaque in latos ierant aequaliter agros,
  inrita decepti vota colentis erant.

diva potens frugum silvis cessabat in altis;
  deciderant longae spicea serta comae.

sola fuit Crete fecundo fertilis anno;
  omnia qua tulerat se dea messis erat.

ipse locus nemorum canebat frugibus Ide
  et ferus in silva farra metebat aper.

optavit Minos similes sibi legifer annos—
  optasset Cereris longus ut esset amor.

qui tibi secubitus tristes, dea flava, fuissent,
  hos cogor sacris nunc ego ferre tuis?

cur ego sim tristis cum sit tibi nata reperta
  regnaque quam Iuno sorte minora regat?

festa dies Veneremque vocat cantusque merumque.
  haec decet ad dominos munera ferre deos.

Witness Crete—Cretans don't always lie.
Crete was the proud nurse of Jove.

There the ruler of the starry sky
was suckled as a tiny baby.

Crete deserves credit—her foster-son supports her.
She knows the facts and Ceres will plead guilty.

In Crete, below Mount Ida, she saw Iasius
the sure marksman hunting fallow-deer—

saw him and felt the flame leap in her heart.
Shame and desire began their tug of war.

Desire won. A drought cracked the fields
and the crops failed.

Though the crooked share had broken the ground
and heavy mattocks pounded the clods,

though the seed was evenly sown in the furrow,
the farmers were cheated, their prayers unanswered.

Deep in the forest the goddess of fruitfulness dallied
and the grain that crowned her long hair fell off.

Only Crete had abundant crops that year—
it was harvest home wherever the goddess trod.

The woods of Ida grew white with wheat
and the wild boar trampled spelt in the forest.

Lawgiver Minos prayed for more such harvests—
he should have prayed for Ceres' love to last.

Golden goddess, you must have hated sleeping alone.
Then why inflict it on me?

Am I to mourn when your long-lost daughter is found
and reigns as queen, second only to Juno?

Surely a festival calls for wine and woman and song?
Surely these are gifts fit for the gods?

xi

Multa diuque tuli. vitiis patientia victa est.
  cede fatigato pectore, turpis Amor.

scilicet adserui iam me fugique catenas,
  et quae non puduit ferre tulisse pudet.

vicimus et domitum pedibus calcamus Amorem.
  venerunt capiti cornua sera meo.

perfer et obdura. dolor hic tibi proderit olim.
  saepe tulit lassis sucus amarus opem.

ergo ego sustinui, foribus tam saepe repulsus,
  ingenuum dura ponere corpus humo?

ergo ego nesciocui quem tu complexa tenebas
  excubui clausam, servus ut, ante domum?

vidi cum foribus lassus prodiret amator,
  invalidum referens emeritumque latus.

hoc tamen est levius quam quod sum visus ab illo—
  eveniat nostris hostibus ille pudor!

quando ego non fixus lateri patienter adhaesi,
  ipse tuus custos, ipse vir, ipse comes?

scilicet et populo per me comitata placebas.
  causa fuit multis noster amoris amor.

turpia quid referam vanae mendacia linguae
  et periuratos in mea damna deos?

quid iuvenum tacitos inter convivia nutus
  verbaque compositis dissimulata notis?

dicta erat aegra mihi—praeceps amensque cucurri,
  veni et rivali non erat aegra meo.

his et quae taceo duravi saepe ferendis.
  quaere alium pro me qui velit ista pati.

To hell with love! I've been a martyr long enough.
You're quite impossible.

I've slipped my shackles. Yes, I'm now a free man—
I can blush to remember how I forgot myself.

Victory at last. I've planted my foot on Cupid's neck.
I didn't know I had it in me.

'Stick to it' I tell myself, 'don't weaken.
It's painful, but think of the pain as medicine.'

Did I really lie down like a tramp on the pavement
all those nights you locked me out?

Did I really stand guard at your door like a slave
while you were hugging another man?

I well remember seeing your lover leave the house
and stagger home—invalided out.

The worst of it was that he saw me—
I could wish my enemies nothing worse.

Was there a single day when I didn't report for duty
as your personal escort, your friend, your lover?

My company made everybody love you.
My passion for you started a male fashion.

I can't forget the lies you fed me,
the promises you fooled me with,

the nods to lover-boys at parties,
the sly remarks in obvious code.

Once, I heard you were ill, rushed to your house in a panic
and found you in bed—yes, in the arms of my rival.

These and other unspeakable insults have made me hard.
Find someone else to play the martyr.

iam mea votiva puppis redimita corona
  lenta tumescentes aequoris audit aquas.
desine blanditias et verba potentia quondam
  perdere—non ego sum stultus ut ante fui.

xib

Luctantur pectusque leve in contraria tendunt
  hac amor hac odium—sed puto vincit amor.
odero si potero. si non, invitus amabo.
  nec iuga taurus amat, quae tamen odit habet.
nequitiam fugio, fugientem forma reducit.
  aversor morum crimina, corpus amo.
sic ego nec sine te nec tecum vivere possum
  et videor voti nescius esse mei.
aut formosa fores minus aut minus improba vellem—
  non facit ad mores tam bona forma malos.
facta merent odium, facies exorat amorem—
  me miserum, vitiis plus valet illa suis!
parce per o lecti socialia iura, per omnes
  qui dant fallendos se tibi saepe deos,
perque tuam faciem, magni mihi numinis instar,
  perque tuos oculos qui rapuere meos!
quicquid eris mea semper eris—tu selige tantum
  me quoque velle velis anne coactus amem.
lintea dem potius ventisque ferentibus utar
  ut quam, si nolim, cogar amare, velim.

My ship's in harbour, garlands hanging from the stern,
deaf to the roar of the rising storm.

Don't waste sweet words and bygone witchery on me.
I've learnt some common sense at last.

xib

Love and hate, here in my heart, at tug of war—
and love I suppose will find a way to win.

I'd sooner hate. If I can't I'll be the reluctant lover—
the dumb ox bearing the yoke he loathes.

Your behaviour drives me away, your beauty draws me back.
I adore your face and abhor your failings.

With or without you life's impossible
and I can't decide what I want.

Why can't you be less lovely or more true?
Why must your faults and your figure clash?

I love what you are and hate what you do—
but your self, alas, outweighs your selfishness.

By the bed we shared, by all the gods
who let you take their names in vain,

by your face my holy icon, by your eyes that ravished mine,
take pity on me.

Be what you will you'll still be mine—but you must choose—
do you want me to want to love you or be forced to?

Make life plain sailing for me please
by helping me love what I can't help loving.

xii

Quis fuit ille dies quo tristia semper amanti
    omina non albae concinuistis aves?

quodve putem sidus nostris occurrere fatis?
    quosve deos in me bella movere querar?

quae modo dicta mea est, quam coepi solus amare,
    cum multis vereor ne sit habenda mihi.

fallimur an nostris innotuit illa libellis?
    sic erit—ingenio prostitit illa meo.

et merito. quid enim formae praeconia feci?
    vendibilis culpa facta puella mea est.

me lenone placet. duce me perductus amator.
    ianua per nostras est adaperta manus.

an prosint dubium, nocuerunt carmina certe—
    invidiae nostris illa fuere bonis.

cum Thebae, cum Troia foret, cum Caesaris acta,
    ingenium movit sola Corinna meum.

aversis utinam tetigissem carmina Musis,
    Phoebus et inceptum destituisset opus!

nec tamen ut testes mos est audire poetas—
    malueram verbis pondus abesse meis.

per nos Scylla patri caros furata capillos
    pube premit rabidos inguinibusque canes.

nos pedibus pinnas dedimus, nos crinibus angues;
    victor Abantiades alite fertur equo.

idem per spatium Tityon porreximus ingens,
    et tria vipereo fecimus ora cani.

fecimus Enceladon iaculantem mille lacertis,
    ambiguae captos virginis ore viros.

AMORES III xii 1–28

xii

Did a raven cross my path one day
and croak bad luck on the eternal lover?

Is some malefic planet opposing me?
Have I antagonized a god?

The girl once mine and only mine
is mine alone no longer.

I suppose my poems made her a public figure?
Yes, my flair commercialized her.

And serve me right. I shouldn't have advertised her beauty.
If she's up for sale it's my own fault.

I've been her pimp, procuring lovers for her,
letting them in at the front door.

I doubt the value of verse. It has certainly done me harm,
making people jealous of my success.

In spite of Thebes and Troy and Caesar's victories
my sole inspiration was Corinna.

If only the Muse had frowned on my first efforts
and Phoebus withdrawn his support.

But after all a poem's not an affidavit—
my statements should have been discounted.

We poets thought up Scylla, who stole her father's curl
and kennels hell-hounds in her womb.

We thought up Hermes' wingèd heels, Medusa's snaky hair,
and Perseus' flying horse.

We elongated that nine acre giant,
gave Cerberus three heads,

Enceladus a thousand whirling arms.
We spellbound heroes with our Siren voices,

Aeolios Ithacis inclusimus utribus Euros;
    proditor in medio Tantalus amne sitit.

de Niobe silicem, de virgine fecimus ursam;
    concinit Odrysium Cecropis ales Ityn.

Iuppiter aut in aves aut se transformat in aurum
    aut secat imposita virgine taurus aquas.

Protea quid referam Thebanaque semina dentes;
    qui vomerent flammas ore fuisse boves;

flere genis electra tuas, auriga, sorores,
    quaeque rates fuerint nunc maris esse deas;

aversumque diem mensis furialibus Atrei,
    duraque percussam saxa secuta lyram?

exit in immensum fecunda licentia vatum,
    obligat historica nec sua verba fide.

et mea debuerat falso laudata videri
    femina. credulitas nunc mihi vestra nocet.

xiii

Cum mihi pomiferis coniunx foret orta Faliscis,
    moenia contigimus victa, Camille, tibi.

casta sacerdotes Iunoni festa parabant
    et celebres ludos indigenamque bovem.

grande morae pretium ritus cognoscere, quamvis
    difficilis clivis huc via praebet iter.

stat vetus et densa praenubilus arbore lucus;
    aspice—concedes numinis esse locum.

accipit ara preces votivaque tura piorum,
    ara per antiquas facta sine arte manus.

huc, ubi praesonuit sollemni tibia cantu,
    it per velatas annua pompa vias.

imprisoned the winds in Odysseus' wine-skin,
tormented Tantalus with eternal thirst,

made flint of Niobe, a she-bear of Callisto,
a mournful nightingale of Philomela,

turned Jupiter to feathers and showers of gold
and bulls in the ocean with virgins on their backs.

Add Proteus, and the Theban dragon's teeth,
fire-breathing oxen,

Phaethon's amber-weeping sisters,
ships transformed to nymphs,

the sun in retreat from Atreus' cannibal feast,
and boulders bowling along to the lilt of the lyre.

In short, poetic licence extends to infinity,
but its documents are unhistorical.

My praise of Corinna should have been read as fiction.
You are my trouble—you, uncritical reader.

xiii

We had come to Falerii, my wife's home,
the orchard town once conquered by Camillus,

and Juno's sisterhood were preparing for her feast—
the crowded games and the sacrifice of a local heifer.

To watch the ritual repays with interest
a trying journey on steep roads.

You reach an ancient grove of thick and gloomy trees
haunted, you feel, by an unseen presence.

Here, at a primitive altar of rough-hewn stone
the faithful offer prayers and incense.

Here, to the music of flutes and plain-chant, every year
a procession comes, through decorated streets

ducuntur niveae populo plaudente iuvencae
    quas aluit campis herba Falisca suis,

et vituli nondum metuenda fronte minaces,
    et minor ex humili victima porcus hara,

duxque gregis cornu per tempora dura recurvo.
    invisa est dominae sola capella deae.

illius indicio silvis inventa sub altis
    dicitur inceptam destituisse fugam.

nunc quoque per pueros iaculis incessitur index
    et pretium auctori vulneris ipsa datur.

qua ventura dea est iuvenes timidaeque puellae
    praeverrunt latas veste iacente vias.

virginei crines auro gemmaque premuntur,
    et tegit auratos palla superba pedes.

more patrum Graio velatae vestibus albis
    tradita supposito vertice sacra ferunt.

ora favent populi tum cum venit aurea pompa,
    ipsa sacerdotes subsequiturque suas.

Argiva est pompae facies. Agamemnone caeso
    et scelus et patrias fugit Halaesus opes,

iamque pererratis profugus terraque fretoque
    moenia felici condidit alta manu.

ille suos docuit Iunonia sacra Faliscos.
    sit mihi, sit populo semper amica suo.

and the crowd's applause, leading snow-white heifers
fattened on Faliscan pasture,

bull calves with danger latent in their foreheads,
pigs—the poor man's offering,

and the lord of the flock, bone-headed, spiral-horned.
Only goats are missing. The goddess hates them.

According to legend, when she ran away from Jove
and hid in the forest a nanny-goat betrayed her.

So now the children throw spears at the tell-tale,
which goes as prize to whoever scores first hit.

Young men and shy girls walk before the goddess,
sweeping the wide street with their trains,

the girls' hair bound with gold and jewels,
their feet gilded, gleaming beneath a stately mantle.

White-robed, in the ancient Greek fashion,
they carry the sacred vessels on their heads,

and the crowd keep silent as Juno passes by
in golden procession behind her sisterhood.

The ritual came from Argos. On Agamemnon's murder
Halaesus fled from his inheritance

and crowned his wanderings over land and sea
by founding these high walls

and teaching his Faliscans the worship of Juno.
May the goddess be gracious—to me and her people, always.

xiv

Non ego ne pecces, cum sis formosa, recuso,
    sed ne sit misero scire necesse mihi.

nec te nostra iubet fieri censura pudicam,
    sed tamen ut temptes dissimulare rogat.

non peccat quaecumque potest peccasse negare,
    solaque famosam culpa professa facit.

quis furor est quae nocte latent in luce fateri
    et quae clam facias facta referre palam!

ignoto meretrix corpus iunctura Quiriti
    opposita populum submovet ante sera.

tu tua prostitues famae peccata sinistrae,
    commissi perages indiciumque tui?

sit tibi mens melior, saltemve imitare pudicas,
    teque probam, quamvis non eris, esse putem.

quae facis, haec facito. tantum fecisse negato.
    nec pudeat coram verba modesta loqui.

est qui nequitiam locus exigat—omnibus illum
    deliciis imple, stet procul inde pudor.

hinc simul exieris, lascivia protinus omnis
    absit, et in lecto crimina pone tuo.

illic nec tunicam tibi sit posuisse pudori
    nec femori impositum sustinuisse femur.

illic purpureis condatur lingua labellis
    inque modos venerem mille figuret amor.

illic nec voces nec verba iuvantia cessent
    spondaque lasciva mobilitate tremat.

indue cum tunicis metuentem crimina vultum
    et pudor obscenum diffiteatur opus.

AMORES III xiv 1-28

xiv

Your loveliness, I don't deny, needs lovers,
but spare me facts and figures—please.

My moral code does not require you to be chaste,
but it does demand concealment.

Any woman who pleads Not Guilty is innocent;
only confession gives her a bad name.

What madness to parade your nightlife in the daylight
and publicize your private affairs!

Even prostitutes insist on privacy
and lock the door before obliging a client.

Will *you* expose your naked guilt to scandalmongers
and give full details of your own misconduct?

Have *some* decency, please—or at least pretend to have,
so I can think you're faithful even if you aren't.

Carry on as before, but don't admit it,
and don't be ashamed of decorum in public.

There's a proper place for impropriety—
enjoy it there, shedding your inhibitions.

But don't forget them when you leave.
Confine your faults to bed.

It's no disgrace to undress there,
press thigh to thigh,

kiss as you please, and figure out
love's total variety,

moaning and whispering sweet words,
shaking the bedstead in abandon.

But when you dress put on your moral make-up too
and wear the negative look of virtue.

da populo. da verba mihi. sine nescius errem
et liceat stulta credulitate frui.

cur totiens video mitti recipique tabellas?
cur pressus prior est interiorque torus?

cur plus quam somno turbatos esse capillos
collaque conspicio dentis habere notam?

tantum non oculos crimen deducis ad ipsos—
si dubitas famae parcere, parce mihi.

mens abit et morior quotiens peccasse fateris,
perque meos artus frigida gutta fluit.

tunc amo, tunc odi frustra quod amare necesse est;
tunc ego—sed tecum—mortuus esse velim.

nil equidem inquiram nec quae celare parabis
insequar, et falli muneris instar erit.

si tamen in media deprensa tenebere culpa
et fuerint oculis probra videnda meis,

quae bene visa mihi fuerint bene visa negato—
concedent verbis lumina nostra tuis.

prona tibi vinci cupientem vincere palma est,
sit modo 'non feci' dicere lingua memor.

cum tibi contingat verbis superare duobus,
etsi non causa, iudice vince tuo.

XV

Quaere novum vatem, tenerorum mater Amorum—
raditur hic elegis ultima meta meis,

quos ego composui Paeligni ruris alumnus
—nec me deliciae dedecuere meae—

si quid id est, usque a proavis vetus ordinis heres,
non modo militiae turbine factus eques.

Take whoever you please—provided you take me in.
Don't enlighten me. Let me keep my illusions.

Need I see those notes coming and going?
That double hollow in the bed?

Your hair in sleepless disarray?
Those love-bites on your neck?

You'll soon be committing adultery before my very eyes.
Destroy your good name if you must, but spare my feelings.

These endless confessions bring me out in a cold sweat—
honestly, they're killing me.

My love becomes frustrated hate for what I can't help loving.
I'd gladly die—if only you'd die with me.

I'll ask no questions, I promise, and ferret out no secrets
if you'll do me the simple favour of deceit.

But if ever I catch you in the act,
if ever I'm forced to see the worst,

then flatly deny I saw what I did,
and your words shall stand in for my eyes.

It's so easy for you to beat a willing loser.
Only remember to say Not Guilty.

Two words can clear you—speak them and win.
Your case may be weak but your judge is weaker.

XV

Mother of the Amorini, my couplets race home,
leaving a vacancy,

and I sign myself 'Pelignian Countryman',
'Respectable Rake',

or, if you like, 'Equestrian of the Fourth Generation'
—no jumped up military knight.

Mantua Vergilio gaudet, Verona Catullo;
    Paelignae dicar gloria gentis ego,

quam sua libertas ad honesta coegerat arma
    cum timuit socias anxia Roma manus.

atque aliquis spectans hospes Sulmonis aquosae
    moenia, quae campi iugera pauca tenent,

'quae tantum' dicet 'potuistis ferre poetam,
    quantulacumque estis, vos ego magna voco.'

culte puer puerique parens Amathusia culti,
    aurea de campo vellite signa meo.

corniger increpuit thyrso graviore Lyaeus—
    pulsanda est magnis area maior equis.

imbelles elegi, genialis Musa, valete,
    post mea mansurum fata superstes opus.

The Mantuans have Virgil, the Veronese Catullus,
but *I* shall be the pride of the Peligni—

freedom-lovers and freedom-fighters
who made imperious Rome afraid.

Picture the future tourist, among these streams,
sizing up Sulmona:

'How tiny to produce a major poet!
I call that great' he'll say.

Child god, and island mother-goddess,
parade your golden banners elsewhere.

The rod of Bacchus reprimands me—
his royal course needs high horses.

Farewell, lively Muse, and unheroic metre,
my labour of love—these immortal remains.

NOTES

These notes are of two kinds—explanatory and textual. I have kept them as few and as short as possible. The textual notes record all variants—excluding punctuation—from E. J. Kenney's Oxford Text. The letters H B M K L refer to the editions of Heinsius (1661), Burman (1727), Munari (4th 1964), Kenney (2nd impression 1965), and Lenz (1965). G refers to G. P. Goold's article 'Amatoria Critica' in *Harvard Studies in Classical Philology* 69 (1965) pp. 1 ff.

The Epigram. The first edition of the *Amores* in five books has disappeared—though there may be traces of it among the variants offered by our extant MSS. The exact date of the second edition in three books is unknown, but it was probably between 11 and 1 B.C. —see the notes on I xiv 45–6 and II xviii 19–20.

BOOK I

i 1   *Arma:* first word of Virgil's *Aeneid.*

2–3   So the two hexameters (12 metrical feet) became hexameter plus pentameter (11 feet), i.e. an elegiac couplet —the usual metre for love poetry.

29   Myrtle was sacred to Venus (Pliny *Natural History* XII 3).

ii 11–12 Ovid took this illustration from Porcius Latro, one of his teachers of rhetoric (Seneca *Controversiae* II ii 8).

24   Mars, Venus's lover, is called Cupid's stepfather at *Am.* II ixb 24. But here Vulcan, Venus's husband, is probably meant. He made arms for Achilles in the *Iliad* and could make a chariot to fit Cupid.

31   *Mens Bona* had a temple on the Capitol (Livy XXIII 32).

48   The nouns can be dative or ablative—(i) 'you drive doves...' (ii) 'you oppress with doves...'

51   The *gens Iulia*, to which Augustus belonged, was named after Iulus the son of Aeneas and traced its descent from Venus, mother of Aeneas and Cupid.

iii 15   *desultor*: trick rider in the circus who jumps from one horse to another.

iv 1   I take *vir* as husband because of the phrase *iure coacta* in line 64. Similarly *Am.* II ii and xix, III iv and viii concern a husband (*maritus*).

5   The Romans, like the Greeks, dined lying down. Three couches, each for three diners, were placed round the table, leaving the fourth side open for service. The trio in this poem recline at the same table—perhaps on the same couch with the woman in the middle.

7–8   At the wedding feast of Pirithous, king of the Lapiths, and Hippodamia, daughter of Adrastus, the Centaurs got drunk and tried to rape the bride (Apollodorus *Epitome* 21).

vi 16   For the pun on *fulmen* cf. II i 20.

25   *umquam* here=‘some time’, as at Quintilian XII ii 9 *utinamque sit tempus umquam quo . . .*

vii 31–2   In an amusing encounter in the *Iliad* (V 330 ff.) the Greek hero Diomedes, son of Tydeus, wounds Aphrodite in the hand with his spear as she tries to rescue Aeneas.

33   *at* suggested by H *et* M K L with the MSS.

55   *aut* my suggestion *ut* H B M K L with the MSS. But ‘as when . . . or . . . or when . . .’ seems more natural than ‘as when . . . as . . . or when . . .’

67   *tristia* has special point because dishevelled hair was a sign of mourning.

182

The name comes from Greek *dipsa* 'thirst'. It was also the name of a poisonous snake and perhaps line 20 alludes to this.

45-6	Literally: 'These women too who crease their brows— examine them closely: things that incriminate can drop out of creases.' Play on *ruga* as (i) 'wrinkle' and (ii) 'fold in a garment' that could be used for hiding stolen objects. Also play on *excute*—'shake out' and 'investigate thoroughly'.

47-8	Allusion to the contest of the bow in *Odyssey* xxi. Penelope promised to marry the suitor who could draw Odysseus' bow and shoot an arrow through twelve axeheads. For *latus* cf. *Am.* III vii 36. *arcus* is used of the phallus in Apuleius *Metamorphoses* II 16.

64	Slaves newly imported from abroad and on sale in the market had their feet coated with gypsum as a distinguishing mark (Pliny *N.H.* XXXV 199).

67	*qui* nearly all the MSS *quin* H M K L. But *quin* introducing a question (M L) normally means 'Why not . . . ?', and introducing a statement in the sense of *immo* doesn't quite fit here.

74	The cult of Isis demanded sexual abstinence at certain times during the year.

84	*illa vel illa* H B *ille vel ille* M K L with most of the MSS.

100	The Via Sacra ran through the Forum and was one of the main shopping centres of ancient Rome.

ix 5	The oldest MSS and H B M K L read *annos*, which repeats the point of the previous couplet. *animos* makes a new one. See G pp. 22-3.

23-4	Allusion to *Iliad* x.

x 30	All MSS read *locanda* 'to be hired' except Y (= *Hamiltonensis* 471 in the Staatsbibliothek, East Berlin) which has the excellent reading *licenda* 'to be bid for'. Recently

Y has been re-dated to the 11th century by Franco Munari—see his monograph *Il Codice Hamilton 471 di Ovidio*, Rome, 1965.

39   The Lex Cincia of 204 B.C. forbade advocates to charge for their services. Augustus re-affirmed this principle round about 17 B.C. (Dio Cassius LIV xviii 2).

49–50   In the time of Romulus Tarpeia betrayed the Capitol to the Sabines in return for what they carried on their left arms; she meant the gold bracelets they wore, but the Sabines interpreted her as meaning their shields and killed her with them (Livy I xi).

51–2   The necklace of Harmonia, daughter of Mars and Venus, brought death on all its owners. With it Polynices bribed Eriphyle to persuade her husband Amphiaraus to join the expedition of the Seven against Thebes. Amphiaraus, having promised to abide by his wife's decision, had to go though he knew he would be killed at Thebes. But before going he made his son Alcmaeon swear to avenge his death by killing Eriphyle (Apollodorus *Bibliotheca* III 60–2).

56   Alcinous, king of Homer's Phaeacians, stands for any rich man. There is a famous description of his orchards in *Odyssey* vii 112–32.

57   *numeret* H B *numerat* M K L. But the subjunctive is needed to balance *conferat*. See G p. 25.

xi 2   *Nape:* Greek name meaning 'glen'.

7   Imagine two schoolboy slates, backed with wood and hinged together at the top so as to face one another, with a coating of wax instead of slate, on which letters could be scratched with a stilus: these were 'double tablets' and when closed they were secured with a clasp and/or seal.

25   Allusion to *litterae laureatae*, a military dispatch bound with bay to report a victory.

26   i.e. he will turn his writing-tablets into votive tablets.

27–8   Literally: 'Naso dedicates his trusty servants to Venus. But not long ago you were cheap maple.'

xiii 3–4   Memnon the Ethiopian, son of Tithonus and Aurora, fought for the Trojans and was killed by Achilles. His tomb in the Troad was said to be visited annually by a flock of birds (probably ruffs) who divided into two troops and fought each other making a blood-offering to Memnon's ghost (Pliny *N.H.* X 74 and D'Arcy W. Thompson *A Glossary of Greek Birds* p. 116).

15   Play on phrase *prima aurora* 'first light' e. g. Livy I vii 6 *ad primam auroram.*

19   Text uncertain. *incautos* Madvig †*cultos*† K *multos* M L. Also uncertain which Atrium is meant.

20   *spondeo* 'I guarantee'.

39   *quem mavis* M *quem manibus* B K L. But hands are not arms—you can't embrace with them. See G pp. 28–9.

43–4   The woman on this occasion was Alcmena, Hercules' mother.

xiv 9–12   Strictly 'cedar' is incorrect for *cedrus* here, because what we call 'cedars' do not grow in the Troad. Ovid's tree is probably our *Juniperus oxycedrus*: its bark separates in long strips—hence *derepto cortice*. The colour meant is auburn. (So Mr Humphrey Gilbert-Carter, former Director of the Cambridge University Botanic Garden.) Ovid had been to the Troad and may be presumed to know what he was talking about.

25   *praebuerunt* B M L *praebuerant* H K. See G p. 29 and M. Platnauer *Latin Elegiac Verse* p. 53.

33–4   The famous Aphrodite Anadyomene of the 4th century Greek painter Apelles, which Augustus had dedicated in the shrine of Julius Caesar (Pliny *N.H.* XXXV 91).

45–6	Drusus defeated the Sygambri in 11 B.C. and was allowed an *ovatio* or minor Triumph (Dio LIV xxxii).
xv 13	The similarity between this and line 8 may hint that Ovid wants to be the Roman Callimachus.
16	Aratus of Soli in Cilicia was a contemporary of Callimachus and wrote a once famous didactic poem on astronomy—the *Phaenomena*.
21	Varro of Atax in Gallia Narbonensis was an elder contemporary of Virgil and wrote an *Argonautica*.
24	Adaptation of Lucretius V 95.
26	Cf. *Aeneid* IX 449.
27	Allusion to Tibullus II vi 15–16.
29	Cornelius Gallus (died 26 B.C.) was the first of the Roman elegiac love poets and this line is probably adapted from him. Lycoris was his pseudonym for the dancer Cytheris.
38	*atque ita* ('and so' i.e. 'wearing my myrtle wreath') M L with all the MSS *atque a* H B K. Ancient books sometimes had a portrait of the author (see Martial I i and XIV clxxxvi). For the ablative of the agent cf. *Met.* ix 624–5.
42	Cf. Horace *Odes* III xxx 6–7 *multaque pars mei/vitabit Libitinam.*

BOOK II

i 12	*satis oris erat:* 'I had the face and the fluency'.
23–8	exploit double meaning of *carmina*—'spells' and 'poems'.
ii 1	*Bagoas:* a Persian name, often given to eunuchs (Pliny *N.H.* XIII 41).
4	Portico of Apollo's temple on the Palatine, with statues of the fifty daughters of Danaus between its columns; see Butler and Barber on Propertius II xxxi.

186

18–27 omitted by oldest MSS but pretty certainly genuine.

iii given as separate poem in the MSS but quite clearly part of ii. The lover now tries the sympathetic approach —with plenty of *double entendre*.

iv 22 Literally: 'I'd like to bear the weight of my critic's thigh.'

v 4 The MSS offer *ei mihi* (H B M K L) and *o mihi*. *in mihi* is Alan Ker's attractive suggestion (*Ovidiana* ed. N. I. Herescu p. 226).—Literally: 'Girl born to be my ever-lasting torment.' See also G pp. 31–2.

vi 30 H B M K L read *poteras*, which makes *ora* a very peculiar accusative of respect. *poterant* has good authority and could have got changed because of *eras* in the hexa-meter.

31–2 follow 25–6 in the MSS. Markland suggested putting them here—see his edition of Statius *Silvae* London 1728 p. 106.

41 Thersites, ugliest of the Greeks at Troy, is described in *Iliad* ii 212 ff.

55 explained by *Ars Amatoria* I 627–8, of which the gist is that peacocks won't display their plumage unless you say nice things about them. In the Birds' Paradise they are less vain.

62 *PLVS AVE:* (i) 'more than a bird' (ii) 'more than *Hail*'. For the iambic shortening cf. *cave*. For the omission of *quam* cf. Hor. *Odes* IV xiv 13 *plus vice simplici*. Martial mentions a parrot that can say *Caesar, ave* (XIV 73).

vii 3 In the Roman theatre the sexes were segregated, the women sitting in the upper rows.

23 *operata* H B M L *operosa* K.

25   *quae tam tibi fida* H B M L *quod erat tibi fida* K.

viii 2   *Cypassis*: Greek name meaning 'Kilty'.

ix 1   Text uncertain. *pro re . . . indignande* Madvig *pro me . . . indignate* ('never angry enough on my behalf') H B M K L. See G pp. 35–6.

9–10   adapt ideas from Callimachus *Epigram* 31.

23   *puella* Burman *puellae* H B M K L. See G pp. 36–7.

ixb   Probably a separate poem, contrasting with ix as viii does with vii. The first line picks up *placide vivere*.

x   Later Ovid addressed three of his *Pontic Letters* to Graecinus, who was consul in A.D. 16.

xi 2   quotes from Catullus lxiv 1 *Peliaco quondam prognatae vertice pinus*.

10   Literally: 'the freezing north wind and the unfreezing south.' According to Seneca *Contr*. II ii 12 Ovid's friends objected to this line but he refused to change it. All MSS of the *Amores* corrupt it; the MSS of Seneca preserve it correctly.

29   Castor and Pollux, protectors of those in danger at sea.

34   Witty adaptation of Propertius I viii 18 *sit Galatea tuae non aliena viae*.

44   *deos*: the image of the ship's guardian god (cf. *Am*. II xvi 28 and *Tr*. I x 1) and also Corinna.

55–6   adapt Tibullus I iii 93–4.

xiv 8   Metaphor from gladiatorial combat in the arena. Sand would be spread on the floor to soak up any blood.

11–12   Deucalion was the Greek Noah. He and his wife Pyrrha survived a world flood and repopulated the earth by throwing stones over their shoulders—see *Metamorphoses* I.

13-14 Thetis was Achilles' mother.

15-16 Romulus and Remus.

17-18 See note on I ii 51.

xv 10 Circe and Proteus.

11 Text uncertain. I print the version argued for by R. P. Oliver in *Classical Philology* 53 (1958) 103 ff. See also G pp. 38-9.

19 K obelizes *si dabor ut condar*. I agree with G and Oliver that it= *si dabor loculis condendus*.

21 *sum* G *sim* H B M K L.

24 *sub gemmam* M L *sub gemma* H B K.

xvi 7 *uvae* H B *uvis* M K L with all MSS. But *ferax* taking different cases in the same line is odd. Influence of *Cereris* and *undis* may have caused the change. Or did Ovid write *Cereri . . . uvis* (cf. *Aetna* 262)?

xvii 24 *toro* (H B) has less authority than *foro* (M K L) but more point. She could lay down the law 'in mid couch' because in the Latin this suggests 'in mid Forum' and because she has not yet admitted him to share her *torus* —cf. I v 2 and II x 18.

xviii 3 Pompeius Macer's lost epic ended where the *Iliad* begins. He was a close friend of Ovid's and related to his third wife (*Ex Ponto* II x).

13-4 refer to Ovid's lost tragedy *Medea*.

19-20 may refer to the *Amores*—the next poem is a good example of *praecepta*. But the *Ars Amatoria* seems more likely—the first edition in two books, certainly published by 1 B.C.

21-6 Ovid published two collections of *Heroides*—I to XV and

XVI to XXI. Nine of the first are mentioned here, including the first letter and the last.
Text of 26 uncertain. See G pp. 42–3.

27–34   Other poems by Sabinus are mentioned in *Ex Ponto* IV xvi 15–16 where we are also told he died young.

38   Protesilaus, Laodamia's newly married husband, was the first of the Greeks to be killed at Troy. The gods allowed him to visit his wife from the underworld and she died in the arms of his ghost (Servius on *Aen.* vi 447).

xix 7   *fortunam* MSS and editors. I risk the conjecture *formosam* which fits *curet* and the pentameter better. For the phrase cf. III iv 41. A scribal reminiscence of Horace *Epistles* I v 12 might have caused the change.

52   *concessa* M *concessi* H B K L. The first is more difficult and has good authority.

BOOK III

i 51–2   follow 45–6 in the MSS. I agree with K's suggestion that they fit better here.

53   *infixa*: see G pp. 54–6. *incisa* H B M K L.

56   *miseram*: see G p. 46. *missam* H B M K L.

ii 15–16   Pelops won the hand of Hippodamia by beating her father the king of Pisa in Elis in a chariot race. Had the king caught him he would have speared him to death. But Hippodamia had bribed the groom to remove the linch-pins from her father's chariot (Apollodorus *Epitome* ix).

18   Taking *quisque* as *uterque*—cf. *Heroides* xix 169.

19–20   *linea*: the seats were marked out by grooves in the stone. At the Circus both sexes sat together; in the Theatre they were segregated (cf. II vii 3).

42	Literally: 'Foul dust, from her fair body go away' (Marlowe).
43	*favete linguis*: ritual formula calling for silence, but the speaker goes rattling on.

iii 17	Text uncertain. *at non invidiae* H B M K L. *sat non . . .* Bentley.
	Andromeda's mother Cassiopea claimed to be more beautiful than the Nereids, and Neptune punished her arrogance by demanding the sacrifice of Andromeda to a sea-monster. She was rescued by Perseus (Apollodorus II 43–4).
39–40	Semele, pregnant with Bacchus, asked Jupiter her lover to appear in all his Olympian glory. Having given his promise Jupiter had to obey and Semele was burnt to death. But he rescued Bacchus and sewed him up in his thigh till the time came for him to be born (Apollodorus III 26–7).

v	The authenticity of this poem is doubtful. For the details see K and his discussion in *Classical Quarterly* 12 (1962) pp. 11–13.
21	Most MSS offer *huc* (H B M K L), some *huic*. Temporal *hic* 'at this point' makes a good connexion and would be very liable to alteration in this context.

vi 13	Perseus.
15–16	Ceres gave Triptolemus a chariot drawn by winged dragons and told him to sow wheat throughout the world.
47–9	Ilia was the mother, by Mars, of Romulus and Remus. Her uncle Amulius ordered the twins to be drowned in the Tiber.
74	*cum* L *dum* H B M K. See G p. 52.

85   *spatiosior undis* Bentley *spatiosus in undis* M K L with the MSS. See G p. 52.

vii 9   *cupide . . . linguis* M L *cupida . . . lingua* K *cupidae . . . linguae* H B.

55   Text uncertain. I follow M K L in obelizing. For a defence of the MS reading see G p. 53.

61–2   Literally: 'What would be the good if Phemius sang to deaf ears? What good would a picture be to poor Thamyras?' Phemius is the minstrel who sings to the suitors in the *Odyssey*, Thamyras a legendary bard blinded by the Muses for daring to compete with them. *iuvet* (62) H B *iuvat* M K L.

viii 29–34   Jupiter turned himself into a shower of gold to seduce Danae in her tower.

ix 4   The tradition that elegy was in origin a lament goes back at least as far as Euripides, who uses the metre for a lament in *Andromache* 103–16 and associates the word with grief at *Iphigenia in Tauris* 146.

5–6   Tibullus died in 19 B.C. or soon after.

23–4   Linos was another legendary son of Apollo. *ailinon* is a Greek cry of grief, said to mean originally *Ah Linos!* When used as an adjective it means 'unhappy'.

29   Text uncertain. The best MSS give *durus optat vatum*, the rest *durat opus vatum* (H B M K L) which implies that Ovid thought the *Iliad* and *Odyssey* were written by different poets. Heinsius proposed *vatis*, Bentley *vati*, G p. 54 *durant, vatis opus*. I hazard *tantum*, which would probably have a double meaning—'only his work' and 'so great a work'.

33–4
and 37   quote from Tibullus I iii 23–6.

40   *tanto* H B *toto* M K L with the MSS. See G pp. 55–6.

47–52   refer to Tib. I iii 3–8—the poet is ill in Phaeacia=
Corcyra=Corfu.

58   adapts Tib. I i 60 *te teneam moriens deficiente manu*,
addressed to Delia.

60   Cf. Tib. I iii 57–8 *sed me . . ./ ipsa Venus campos ducet in
Elysios.*

61–4   Calvus and Catullus had written elegiacs some forty
years earlier. Gallus (see note on I xv 29), friend of
Augustus, was deprived of his governorship of Egypt,
banished, and committed suicide in 26 B.C.

x 9   *quercus . . . prima*: reference to the sacred oak of Zeus at
Dodona in Epirus, the most ancient Greek oracle.

19   'The Cretans are always liars, evil beasts, slow bellies'
Pauline *Epistle to Titus* i 12; the Greek original is a hexameter by the Cretan philosopher poet Epimenides (6th
century B.C.).

45   Proserpina, kidnapped by Pluto on the plain of Enna
and made his queen in the Underworld. For six months
of each year she returned to her mother.

xi 6   'At last my head has sprouted horns'—*cornua* sym-
bolizing strength and courage.

xib   Probably a separate poem, like II ixb.

20   *ut* H B M L *et* K.

xiii 29   *ora* Madvig *ore* H B M K L. Plural *populi* (cf. 13 and 36)
awkward here—especially as *ore favet populus* possible.
See G pp. 56–7.

36   *sit . . . sit* M L (understanding Juno from *Iunonia*) *sint
. . . . sint* H B K.

xv 2   *hic* H B M L *haec* K.

4   *deliciae*: (i) sensuality (ii) light verse (*Tr.* II 78) (iii)
darling (Catullus xxxii 2).

9-10   The Pelignians played a leading part in the Social War
        of 91–87 B.C. Their town Corfinium was made the
        allied capital and renamed Italia. The war compelled
        the Senate to grant full citizenship to Rome's Italian
        allies.

17-18   announce Ovid's intention to write a tragedy, Bacchus
        being patron god of drama.

THE POET

Ovid is the only classical poet to have written an autobiography—*Tristia* IV x, a poem of sixty-six elegiac couplets, composed in exile during the winter of A.D. 10/11 and addressed to Posterity. But of course he could not foresee the 20th century and he was fettered by his medium and his situation, so his verses raise almost as many questions as they answer. Still, thanks to this poem, to passages from several others, and to some bits of information from the elder Seneca, we know quite a lot about his life.

He always refers to himself as Naso (his family name), probably because the only form of Ovidius (his gentile name) manageable in dactylic verse is the vocative and contracted genitive *Ovidi*. The MSS report his first name as Publius.

He was a Pelignian, from Sulmo, a small town some ninety miles east of Rome in a fertile valley of the Apennines, and he describes his home country in *Amores* II xvi.

He records the year of his birth as the year 'when Fate struck both consuls down'. We call it 43 B.C., the year after Caesar's murder, when Hirtius and Pansa died at Mutina, fighting for the Senate against Mark Antony.

His ancestors, for several generations, had been Roman knights, and he took pride in his inherited equestrian rank. But he was a second son; there was a brother one year older and by a curious coincidence they shared the same birthday—'the second day of Minerva's festival' or by our reckoning 20th March.

Their middle-aged father (at least forty when Ovid was born) sent the boys to Rome to be educated. The staple of this education was Greek and Latin literature followed by rhetoric, or training in public speaking, again in both Greek and Latin. The elder Seneca mentions the names of two of Ovid's teachers of rhetoric—Arellius Fuscus from Asia Minor and Porcius Latro from Spain—and quotes an example of his declamation, remarking that his prose style at that time could best be described as free verse. Elsewhere Ovid tells us that he went as a student to Athens—no doubt to study philosophy—and travelled with his friend the poet Macer, visiting the cities of Asia Minor and the site of Troy, and spending almost a year in Sicily.

To return to *Tristia* IV x. At the age of sixteen or seventeen the two brothers were given the right to wear the *latus clavus* or broad purple stripe; in other words Augustus chose them, with other promising sons of equestrian families, as candidates for the senatorial *cursus honorum*, the public career which would give them senatorial rank. But Ovid's brother died at the age of twenty, and Ovid himself, having held two minor magistracies, decided to give up politics for poetry. He could at this time have gone on to the quaestorship and become a senator—the first Pelignian senator, in fact—but he tells us he had no political ambition and public life would have taken up too much of his time. So he 'narrowed his purple stripe' and remained a knight, thereby perhaps incurring, for the first but not the last time, the displeasure of the Princeps.

He began to give public readings of his poetry 'when his beard had been trimmed once or twice'. It was elegiac love poetry in the tradition of Tibullus and Propertius, celebrating a girl he calls Corinna—a pseudonym like Delia and Cynthia but in this case we do not know her real name. She was tall and slim, with long auburn hair, pale complexion and flashing eyes (*Am.* I v 22, viii 35, xiv 9–12, III iii 3–9)—the pre-Raphaelite type.

Ovid regrets that the early death of Tibullus prevented them becoming friends but implies that he knew Propertius well. He did not, however, belong to the circle of Maecenas; his patron was Messalla, who was also the patron of Tibullus. He must have published his first collection of love poems about 23 B.C. Four more appeared at intervals and together they made up the first edition of his *Amores* in five books. The extant *Amores* are the second, revised edition (see p. vii). The work was a best-seller.

Surprisingly, he mentions in this autobiography none of the poetry he published after the *Amores* and before the *Tristia*, though it amounts to many thousands of lines and includes some of his finest work. For all we are told here the *Heroides*, *Medea* (his lost tragedy), *Ars Amatoria*, *Remedia Amoris*, *Metamorphoses* and *Fasti* might never have been written.

He continues with a few personal details. He adored women and fell in love easily, but avoided all scandal—which means, he was never known to have committed adultery with the wife of a Roman citizen (*Trist.* II 349-52). He married three times. He had one daughter, who married twice and gave him two grand-children. Her second husband was Cornelius Fidus, famous for having burst into tears in the Senate when Corbulo referred to him as 'that depilated ostrich' (Seneca the Younger *Dialogus* II 17). The poet's father lived to be ninety, but both his parents, he gratefully records, died before his banishment.

This disaster struck him at the age of fifty. In A.D. 8 by imperial edict he was 'relegated' to Tomis on the Black Sea. There was no trial and no appeal; the legal basis of the edict was probably the emperor's *imperium*. Ovid gives two reasons for his banishment— *carmen et error* 'a poem and a mistake'. The poem was his *Ars Amatoria*, first published at least eight years before—about the time Augustus banished his own daughter Julia for adultery. It is important to remember that Augustus, himself no moral paragon, had made adultery a criminal offence by the promulgation, some twenty years before, of the *Lex Iulia de adulteriis coercendis*.

As for the 'mistake' it remains an enigma. What is certain is that Ovid had been the eye-witness of a serious offence (*crimen*) which directly concerned the Princeps. The fact that the younger Julia, Augustus's granddaughter, was exiled for adultery in the same year as Ovid lends support to the idea that he was somehow involved in her misconduct. Her lover, Decimus Junius Silanus, though not actually banished, was forbidden the imperial presence and withdrew (no doubt wisely) into voluntary exile, where he remained till A.D. 20, when Tiberius allowed him to return to Rome. Julia was less fortunate, exiled till her death in A.D. 28. Ovid too died in exile, still at Tomis, in A.D. 18.

Why was he sent to this remote and barbarous outpost of the Roman Empire? It is difficult to avoid the conclusion that he was, quite simply, a victim of the emperor's personal spite. The fashionable poet whose most popular work could be regarded by critics as a direct incitement to adultery, had hardly furthered the Augustan reformation or deserved well of the 'restored Republic'.

He ends his autobiography with a tribute to his Muse, thanking her for guidance and consolation, ascribing to her his world-wide popularity, and prophesying that his work would live. He was right. The Princeps could not prevent it, though he banished the poet and banned his poems from the public libraries.*

* For further information consult H. Fränkel *Ovid: a Poet between Two Worlds* J. C. Thibault *The Mystery of Ovid's Exile* and L. P. Wilkinson *Ovid Recalled* (in paperback: *Ovid Surveyed*).

THE TRANSLATION

Seven years ago I thought I could do a fairly literal translation of the *Amores* into modern English, but a long struggle with the first few poems convinced me that the letter kills.

Literal translation can be totally misleading. Usually the tone is all wrong. Take the opening couplet. H. T. Riley in 1896 thought the literal 'meaning' was this:

I was preparing to write of arms and impetuous warfare in serious numbers, the subject-matter being suited to the measure.

But it is inconceivable that this is what the poet 'means'. He means he meant to write an epic, in hexameters, the regular epic metre from Homer onwards, but he does not mean it seriously. He means the reader to think of the *Aeneid*. He means to sound grandiose, undercutting epic dignity by the dactylic movement of the whole couplet. He means a slight pun on *edere*, which suggests among other things 'give birth to'. He also means to be epigrammatic and literary-critical—*materia conveniente modis*. And when all this has been said his poetic 'meaning' is still not exhausted. No translator has a hope of getting it all in. So I took as my motto the Greek proverb *pleon hemisu pantos* 'half is more than all', kept the translation line for line and tried above all to catch the spirit and persuade the reader to go on reading. A rhetorical problem.

There are certain effects that can only be got in an inflected language. Take the fourth couplet of *Am.* I i:

quid si praeripiat flavae Venus arma Minervae,
ventilet accensas flava Minerva faces?

Imagine Venus grabbing blonde Minerva's armour,
blonde Minerva brandishing a burning torch.

The repeated Latin adjective has point because it rings a change of case and chimes pleasantly with its noun. One cannot represent this in English and it might as well go. *Accensas* too has point because it balances the line; placed half-way it anticipates and is clinched by its noun *faces* at the end. This word order cannot be reproduced in an uninflected language and the adjective is not essential to the meaning; on the other hand the modern reader needs to know that the torch is love's, without having to stop and work it out for himself. So I omit the decoration and make an implication explicit.

Sometimes it is more effective to recast the form of the Latin entirely, as at *Am.* I iii 5–6:

> accipe per longos tibi qui deserviat annos,
> accipe qui pura norit amare fide

> Take a man who can be your slave through the long years,
> take a man who knows how to love truly.

This is flat and longwinded. Nothing essential is lost by cutting it down:

> I'll be your slave for life,
> your ever faithful lover.

This cutting down is the converse of the filling in familiar to composers of Latin elegiacs. For example, Thomas Carew's lines

> He that loves a rosy cheek
> Or a coral lip admires

were turned into Ovidian elegiacs by H. A. J. Munro like this:

> cui facies cordi roseos imitata colores
> labrave curalii tincta rubore placent

> He who loves a face that imitates the colour of the rose
> or admires lips dyed with the blush of coral.*

So if scholars find my version too free at any point, I would ask them to sit down to the problem of translating it back into Ovidian ele-

---

* One should not deduce from this that Latin is a ponderous language; it is simply un-English. The Latin here contains the same number of words as Carew's lines though more than twice as many syllables.

200

giacs and consider the Latin from that point of view before pronouncing judgement.

It remains to defend the choice of free verse. The Ovidian couplet —dactylic hexameter plus pentameter with disyllabic ending—is a tight verse-form with strict rules. Should not a translator represent it by a correspondingly strict English form? The obvious choice, our so-called heroic couplet, has two disadvantages: it lacks the variety of elegiacs and is haunted by the ghosts of Dryden and Pope—not to mention the Pantomime Good Fairy. Other possibilities are an alexandrine plus a pentameter, or two pentameters (the first with a feminine ending). Both have the advantage of being relatively fresh but both are likely to become monotonous in the long run—and the *Amores* contain more than twelve hundred and thirty couplets. Besides they would make it impossible to cut down the Latin. So in the end I left myself free to use not only these two combinations but a variety of others, often in one and the same poem, hoping this would make for liveliness and greater readability.

ACKNOWLEDGEMENTS

I wish to thank the Delegates of the Clarendon Press and Mr E. J. Kenney for kind permission to use his Oxford Text of the *Amores* as the basis for my own (all departures from it are recorded in the Notes); Dr Walter Marg for the idea of spacing out the couplets; Mr W. A. Camps and Mr Kenney for discussion of textual problems; Mr J. A. Crook for Roman legal and historical advice; Mr L. P. Wilkinson for reading and criticizing an earlier version of this translation; and Helen Lee for patience, help and encouragement over many years.